# PSALM 40

## CRYING OUT TO THE GOD WHO DELIGHTS TO RESCUE US

### SARAH MAE

LifeWay Press®
Nashville, Tennessee

Published by LifeWay Press®
© 2019 Sarah Mae Hoover

Author's literary agent is D.C. Jacobson & Associates LLC, an Author Management Company, www.dcjacobson.com.

ISBN: 978-1-4627-9684-7
Item: 005802348
Dewey decimal classification: 248.843
Subject heading: WOMEN / BIBLE. O.T. PSALMS 40 / GOD

To order additional copies of this resource, write LifeWay Church Resources Customer Service; One LifeWay Plaza; Nashville, TN 37234; Fax order to 615.251.5933; call toll-free 800.458.2772; email orderentry@lifeway.com; order online at www.lifeway.com; or visit the LifeWay Christian Store serving you.

Printed in Canada.

Adult Ministry Publishing, LifeWay Church Resources, One LifeWay Plaza, Nashville, TN 37234

EDITORIAL TEAM,
ADULT MINISTRY
PUBLISHING

Michelle Hicks
Manager, Adult Ministry
Short Term Bible Studies

Sarah Doss
Content Editor

Lindsey Bush
Production Editor

Heather Wetherington
Art Director

Chelsea Waack
Graphic Designer

Alexis Ward
Cover Design

# CONTENTS

# ABOUT THE AUTHOR

Sarah Mae is the author of several books, including *The Complicated Heart: Loving Even When It Hurts* and *Desperate: Hope for the Mom Who Needs to Breathe* (with Sally Clarkson). She is also the host of the *The Complicated Heart* Podcast (sarahmae.com/thecomplicatedheartpodcast), a podcast for those looking for healing in the pain and restoration in the ruins.

She resides in Lancaster County, Pennsylvania, with her husband, her three children, and their yellow lab, Memphis.

You can find her online at sarahmae.com and on Instagram® at Instagram.com/sarahmaewrites.

Follow the Psalm 40 conversation on Instagram using the hashtag: #Psalm40Stories

# INTRODUCTION

## THE UNDERCURRENT OF PAIN AND PRAISE

Welcome to this study of Psalm 40! I am filled up with gratefulness to walk these words with you over the next several weeks. It is my prayer that through this study we would learn how to be gut-honest before God and others, believe that He cares about our pain and desires and delights to delivers us, and that we would become unwavering in our trust in Him.

Let me share some backstory on how this study came about.

When God shifts the entire course of your life, all you want to do is tell people about what He did, who He is, and how He can shift your life in a profoundly life-changing, world-rocking way.

God rocked my world through a steady, gentle wooing that all culminated in giving my life to Him in my teens. I remember the wooing, the crisp memories of Him intervening in my life as if to say, "I'm here. I love you, and I'm waiting for you." By the time I was in high school and the Bible was coming alive to me—thanks to the leading and influence of Young Life® leaders—I became *that* girl, the one who tells everyone about Jesus because she thinks no one knows about Him. She thinks, if they did know about Him, they would drop everything and run to Him as fast as they could.

I discovered quickly that not everyone who heard about Jesus shared my enthusiasm. Many of my friends and family just weren't interested. I didn't understand why they wouldn't want to be loved by the God of the universe, who has the power to change their lives.

Now I see, years later after experiencing deep pain, loss, confusion, doubt and heartache, that so often pain steps in the way, hardening us against being tender and vulnerable enough to allow God the opportunity to love us and heal us. To believe God is to risk. But to live an honest life is to risk, and in that risk is the undulating undercurrent of both pain and praise.

We Christians choose risk. And yet, we still struggle to let God love us and heal us in the places where our secrets and fears and insecurities and anger sit. Sometimes we fear disappointment, that God won't really come through for us or those we love. Sometimes we're angry at life's circumstances and unfair dealings. We're not sure if we can really trust God, at least not up-close, not intimately, because if we do, maybe He'll fail us. It's easier to stay on the surface of things, get by, keep going. Or maybe, we think, He's not even really there and our prayers are just blowing breath to the wind.

The thing is, many of us reading this study have experienced God in a world-rocking way. We've known Him in the darkest nights. We've seen Him work in our lives. We've watched Him answer the cries of those who have desperately cried out for help, some of those cries being our own. We love Him. We know Him. And yet, we still allow locked-up places in our hearts—places we're not sure we can let Him or others into. We pretend we're fine until our lives become fine and getting by is enough. But we're not fine. We have secrets, things we don't want people to know, the true things that if we said them out loud we might be judged or rejected.

What would happen if people knew the things we're each struggling with? Things like:

- My fear and anxiety cripple me some days.
- My life didn't turn out the way I wanted it to.
- My past is full of pain and choices I regret.
- I can't shake this sin. I struggle with it over and over.
- I don't know if I even believe in God—that He's real or that I can really trust Him.

Life is full and surprising and often, confusing. It's not just full of joy and beauty and crisp Autumn air, baby-head smells, stories that invade our hearts, sunshine, ocean waves, mountain splendor, sugary lattes, and those wonderfully warm and fuzzy feelings in our tummies that overwhelm in the best of ways; it's full of mundane days, gut-wrenching loss, quiet desperation, unexpected diagnoses, secret pain, and unhealed wounds. And the question arises, *Where are You in all of this, God?* More questions follow: *Do You hear my cries for help? Do You even care? Can I really trust You?*

Psalm 40 is an answer to these questions.

The psalmist-poets ask the same questions we ask, and they cry out in the same ways we cry out: desperately seeking relief and help. The cries of the psalmists are guttural, honest, and real. "Poets use words to drag us into the depth of reality itself."[1] Aren't we all dying to be a little more real and to be around people who are honest in the "depth of reality"? Psalm 40 serves us with an example of how to cry out in the midst of our deepest pain and questions.

Yet, it's also a call to remember God's faithfulness, to recall the truth in the pain, and to know that God hears our prayers and delights to deliver us. He gives new songs to parched lips.

This psalm, specifically verses 1-3, has been a lifeline to me for more than ten years, and I believe it will become one for you as well. None of us who are about to enter into this study are exempt from pain and sin. You might know exactly what your cry for help is, or you might not know, but since you're not dead we know God is still working in you for your good. Praise Him!

*Lord, help us all to come before You and Your Word with a surrendered heart, humble and willing to listen and obey. Amen.*

Let's open ourselves up now to that good and holy and gentle work.

I'm with you all the way.

Your Sister in Christ,

# *HOW TO USE THIS STUDY*

I'm so grateful that you've decided to join me in this study of Psalm 40. I pray that as God leads us in this journey through Scripture, He will bind up our wounds, give us new songs, delight us with His goodness, and reveal beautiful truths from His Word that change our hearts and minds.

In each session, you'll find a group discussion guide and four sections of personal study. I have broken each session into sections. Sometimes we can get tripped up thinking we need to complete the study on the day it says, and that can feel overwhelming, especially if we get behind. With four sections, you can choose when and how long you spend on each section—completing all of them at once, or a little each day, according to your personality and schedule.

## GROUP GUIDES

If you meet with a small group of women to study together, feel free to use these questions to guide your time. I've included the Group Guides before each session's personal study time. I've intentionally crafted these Group Guides to briefly review the previous session's personal study at the beginning of your time together, and then to transition to the new topic for the following week.

This study is intended for groups to meet together first, review last session's personal study, discuss a brief introduction to the next session's topic, including the video teaching if you'd like, and then take the following week to study the topic on your own.

For reference, here's a sample schedule for the order of your first week of *Psalm 40*.

- ☐ Meet in your group and follow the order of the Group Guide on page 12.
- ☐ In the week following your first group meeting, complete the personal study on pages 14–29 before your second group meeting.

In this study, we'll spend time diving into the meaning of Psalm 40 and themes that arise from our study time. There are a few things you'll need to know as you begin:

- □ Optional videos are available to introduce each session. These videos will allow us to get to know one another better and give you a bit more context as you begin each session's study. If you haven't already done so, feel free to buy the videos at LifeWay.com/Psalm40.
- □ In our time together, in the videos and personal study, I share some of my own stories with you. I want to "go first," since I'm asking you to be vulnerable and honest throughout this study. I don't believe that my story is my own; I will tell of who God is and what's He's done in my life, and I encourage you to do the same.
- □ In this study, we're going to ask some pretty honest questions of ourselves and of the Bible. Especially in group discussion times, my prayer is for real, honest community to develop, in which women can share what's really happening in their lives without having to worry about how they will appear. With this in mind, let's work hard to develop a culture of trust and honesty in these group times. Be sure to keep confidential the things shared within the group time together. Listen to your small group friends with care. If you sense one of the group members is in a dangerous, unhealthy, or abusive situation, please reach out to church leadership and/or the appropriate governmental authorities.
- □ As we ask these hard questions of ourselves, some deeper emotional and spiritual wounds may be unearthed. Some of the women in your group may be dealing with issues that require help from outside sources. If you sense that a woman may need more extensive help and support than your group can offer, the leader of the group should refer her to speak with your pastor or a trained Christian counselor. Make sure that your group cares for her well too, following up to check in with her. Be sensitive to the Holy Spirit's leading as you love and offer hope to the women in your group.

My hope is that this Bible study will remind you of how much God loves you and desires an intimate relationship with you. I can't wait to see what He does in and through our lives in this time together. Let's get to it!

# SESSION ONE:

# GETTING OUR HANDS INTO THE DIRT OF PSALM 40

I waited patiently for the LORD;
he inclined to me and heard my cry.
He drew me up from the pit of destruction,
out of the miry bog,
and set my feet upon a rock,
making my steps secure.
He put a new song in my mouth,
a song of praise to our God.
Many will see and fear,
and put their trust in the LORD.

**PSALM 40:1-3**

# GROUP GUIDE

## WARM THINGS UP

Ask everyone in your group to answer the following questions. We want to begin building community and honesty from the first group meeting!

What made you decide to be a part of this study?

Name a few hopes and expectations you have for the study.

Do you enjoy reading the Psalms? Why or why not?

Many of the psalms are meant to be sung as songs. What's your favorite song that you sing in church?

## WATCH

To view Session One's teaching from Sarah Mae, download the optional video bundle at LifeWay.com/Psalm40.

## CREATE CONVERSATION

In the Psalms, God allows us to see the psalmists' real feelings, their processing of good and bad, and their crying out to God. Why do you think God gave us the Psalms? Brainstorm a few possibilities.

Do you find it easy or difficult to be honest with God about your struggles, hopes, and desires? Explain.

Do you find it easy or difficult to be honest with others in the church about your struggles, hopes, and desires? Explain.

How do you react when others are honest with you about what's really happening in their lives? How do you hope others will react when you're honest? Explain.

Read Psalm 119:18 and Luke 24:45 aloud. Take a few moments to pray those passages of Scripture back to God, asking Him to open your eyes to understand His Word and to change your hearts by its power.

_____

_____

_____

_____

_____

_____

_____

_____

_____

_____

_____

_____

_____

_____

_____

_____

_____

_____

_____

_____

_____

_____

_____

_____

_____

_____

# DURING THIS SESSION, I WANT US TO GET OUR HANDS AND HEARTS INTO THE DIRT OF PSALM 40.

## What on earth do I mean when I say that?

When I use the word *hand*, I'm talking about our minds, what we can *grasp*. Our minds want to understand; they want facts. When I say *heart* I'm talking about our emotions, how the truth of the Scriptures connects to places *not* grasped, but rather felt and sensed and engaged on a level outside of understanding.

We're called to love God with our minds and our hearts (Luke 10:27), to love with understanding and with "the *affective* center of our being."[1] In fact, God wants us to persevere as we love Him with our minds and emotions, pushing through when it's hard and when it hurts, when there's resistance and when there's mediocrity. I'm asking us to approach the Scripture willing to use our minds to think and see, and allowing our hearts to be vulnerable as we go forward in our learning.

And what of dirt? Isn't dirt messy and—*dirty*? Why would I use that word?

First, *dirt* is not a dirty word. Dirt is earthy and foundational; it births life. God breathed into it, creating us and gently forming us from dust into daughter. There's something about dirt, the place of formation, where even in the mess God does something new. My hope is that as we interact with Psalm 40, we will find newness in the places we thought were dead or dying, hopeless or abandoned.

To get into the dirt is to reach down, dig our hands in, and see what we can find—to see what's buried that's just waiting to be discovered.

We're going to get our hands and our senses and our minds and our hearts into Psalm 40. We're going to give ourselves to the whole psalm with an inductive focus in mind—in other words, with our ability to reason it out carefully and honestly as we observe the text, the prayer of a real person, and look for the meaning and intention of the author, what he can teach us, and how it relates to us and applies to our lives. We're going to look at words and passages and metaphors, asking questions along the way, and letting it take us where the Holy Spirit leads. We're going to engage our imaginations and our senses, remembering that the Psalms are not some scholarly work to be dissected in a detached manner, but rather an example on how to approach our Father God without pretense.

At the end of the first week, you'll be familiar with the whole psalm.

Psalm 40:1-3 is what I call, "The Redemption Rhythm of God." These three verses are the crying out to God, His saving of us, and His continued work in our lives as we live by faith and tell others the good news. God gives us a rhythmic cycle of redemption in these poetic words. Over and over and over again through all generations and all time, the gospel is at work. God hears; He saves, and He gives a new song for us to sing to all who will listen. We are participants in this rhythm, because not only is our saving "once and done," but it continues in God's work in our every day, in the ordinary ups and downs of our lives, in our sanctification, and in our coming to look more like Him.

These three verses are also an overview of the rest of Psalm 40. Our study is going to be primarily based on the redemption rhythm verses, how they connect to the rest of the psalm, and how the themes presented therein apply to our lives. Because the biblical story of God is a vast tapestry of God's interactions with humanity, we can't help but let the psalm lead us into the rest of the story to see what God would teach us through the fullness of His Word. All to say, we'll be studying a lot of Scripture.

With our hands and our hearts, let's dig in.

¹ I waited patiently for the LORD;
he inclined to me and heard my cry.
² He drew me up from the pit of destruction,
out of the miry bog,
and set my feet upon a rock,
making my steps secure.
³ He put a new song in my mouth,
a song of praise to our God.
Many will see and fear,
and put their trust in the LORD.

⁴ Blessed is the man who makes the LORD his trust,
who does not turn to the proud,
to those who go astray after a lie!
⁵ You have multiplied, O LORD my God,
your wondrous deeds and your thoughts toward us;
none can compare with you!
I will proclaim and tell of them,
yet they are more than can be told.

⁶ In sacrifice and offering you have not delighted,
but you have given me an open ear.
Burnt offering and sin offering you have not required.
⁷ Then I said, "Behold, I have come;
in the scroll of the book it is written of me:
⁸ I delight to do your will, O my God;
your law is within my heart."

⁹ I have told the glad news of deliverance
in the great congregation;
behold, I have not restrained my lips,
as you know, O LORD.

¹⁰ I have not hidden your deliverance within my heart;
I have spoken of your faithfulness and your salvation;
I have not concealed your steadfast
love and your faithfulness
from the great congregation.

¹¹ As for you, O Lord, you will not
restrain your mercy from me;
your steadfast love and your faithfulness will
ever preserve me!
¹² For evils have encompassed me beyond number;
my iniquities have overtaken me,
and I cannot see;
they are more than the hairs of my head;
my heart fails me.

¹³ Be pleased, O Lord, to deliver me!
O Lord, make haste to help me!
¹⁴ Let those be put to shame and disappointed
altogether who seek to snatch away my life;
let those be turned back and brought to
dishonor who delight in my hurt!
¹⁵ Let those be appalled because of their
shame who say to me, "Aha, Aha!"

¹⁶ But may all who seek you rejoice and be glad in you;
may those who love your salvation say
continually, "Great is the Lord!"
¹⁷ As for me, I am poor and needy, but
the Lord takes thought for me.
You are my help and my deliverer;
do not delay, O my God!

## PSALM 40

**(1)**

# *OUR FIRST LOOK AT THE TEXT*

… he inclined to me
and heard my cry.

**PSALM 40:1b**

Look up these Scriptures:

Psalm 119:18

Luke 24:45

With these verses in mind, what two requests can we make to God before we read Psalm 40 (or engage in any Scripture reading)?

1.

2.

Before you begin your reading, pray with me:

*Father, thank You for giving me the Scriptures. Would You open my mind to understand and my eyes to see wondrous, extraordinary things from the passage of Scripture before me? Remove any hindrance that stands between me and Your Word, and uncover and reveal what You want me to see. Teach me to delight in Your Word. Thank You for who You are and how You love me. In Jesus' name I pray. Amen.*

The first thing you're going to do in this session is read Psalm 40 in its entirety two times. Read it once in your head and once out loud. When you read out loud you are more likely to remember the material. You are *not* studying right now. Do not read in a scholarly or searching fashion. Read the passage for what it is: a prayer. See if you can enter into the prayer-poem and allow yourself to feel what the psalmist felt. Have you ever felt desperate for God to help you? Have you ever experienced His mercy? Desperation and mercy, pain and praise, that is the atmosphere of Psalm 40. Enter into it.

Read Psalm 40, which we've provided for you on pages 16–17.

## OBSERVATION: GETTING STARTED

Now that you've read Psalm 40 twice, let's dive into our study.

The guiding question in biblical observation is, *What does the Scripture say?* That question leads us to ask, *When I look at the text, what do I see?*

Let's get started by answering some foundational questions about Psalm 40. (When approaching a biblical text in study for the first time, it's helpful to use basic questions like: Who? What? When? Where? Why?)

Who wrote Psalm 40? (Notice the note above v. 1 in your Bible.)

Who was the psalm written for? (Notice the note above v. 1 in your Bible.)

What's a choirmaster? (Feel free to look this up in the dictionary.)

Why might this psalm have been written for the choirmaster?
(Hint: who would have benefited from it? See v. 9.)

Why do you think David would share his most honest and vulnerable thoughts and prayers with an assembly, or congregation, of believers?

The Psalms were compiled into the book we have today *for* the congregation, for others to hear and pray and sing, learning how to pray and finding intimacy with God and kinship and encouragement with others through honest and vulnerable poetic prayers in community.

Have you ever shared (or would you share) your most honest and vulnerable thoughts and prayers with a group of other believers? Why or why not?

# 2

# *MAKING THE STUDY OUR OWN*

Before we begin, pray a prayer like this:

*Father God, open my mind so that I may understand the Scriptures, and my eyes that I may behold wondrous things in Your Word.*

## STEP ONE: *MAKE YOUR INITIAL OBSERVATIONS.*

Read Psalm 40 again (see pp. 16–17). This time highlight *anything* that stands out to you or is interesting or factual. Feel free to use different color highlighters or pens. Circle words or phrases that stand out to you; put question marks next to phrases or words you don't understand, and mark up the page as you like. As questions come up, embrace them—even the hard questions. This is a fun first step in getting familiar with Psalm 40.

The more you read the psalm and the more curious you are, the more questions you will have. Questions lead to study, and study leads to insight!

Record your observations and questions in the space provided on the next page or in your journal. Feel free to add to these pages as more observations and questions surface.

## STEP TWO: LOOK FOR REPEATED OR RELATED WORDS AND PHRASES.

Look for "things emphasized, things repeated, things related, things alike, things unlike, and things that are true to life."[2] List out words and phrases that are repeated (for example, "… your steadfast love and faithfulness" v. 10b; "… your steadfast love and faithfulness" v. 11b).

List words and phrases that seem related or share similar ideas and themes (for example, "… your thoughts toward us …" v. 5b; "… the Lord takes thought for me …" v. 17).

Look at verses 1-3. Circle the word "I" and the word "my" everywhere you see them. Circle the word "He" everywhere you see it.

Who cries out to the Lord?

Who waits?

Who draws us up out of the pit of destruction?

Who sets our feet on a rock?

Who puts a new song in our mouths?

After answering the previous questions, write down what your role is and what God's role is when it comes to your redemption.

My role (what I do):

God's role (what God does):

Feel free to continue this observational approach and exercise through the whole psalm, recording your notes in a journal.

## STEP THREE: LOOK FOR IMAGERY.

First, a note about Hebrew poetry. Poetry, specifically Hebrew poetry, is the language of the Psalms (every psalm is a poem), and so it seems important that we have at least a basic understanding of what that means.

In considering Hebrew poetry, it's important to understand its use of metaphor ("The LORD is my rock," Ps. 18:2) and simile ("But I have calmed and quieted my soul, like a weaned child with its mother," Ps. 131:2). We also want to be aware of a device called, parallelism, a structure of thought that has intentional contrast, repetition, comparison, or uses two phrases to serve as complements for one another to add to their meaning. Let's look at a few examples to further our understanding.

**SIMILAR:** "The cords of death encompassed me; the torrents of destruction assailed me" (Ps. 18:4).

**CONTRASTING:** "The tongue of the wise commends knowledge, but the mouths of fools pour out folly" (Prov. 15:2).

**COMPARATIVE/COMPLEMENTARY (EMBLEMATIC PARALLELISM):** "As a deer pants for flowing streams, so pants my soul for you, O God" (Ps. 42:1).

Remember, imagery and illustrative language represent a concept, naming something tangible to explain the intangible. For example, in Psalm 40:2b David said that God "… set my feet upon a rock …" A rock is a tangible object we can picture and see and feel to help us understand the concept that God gives us a firm foundation, one on which our feet won't slip and where we can be secure.

List all the imagery you see in Psalm 40.

If you have time, write a few metaphors or illustrative phrases of your own that communicate the same ideas you've found in Psalm 40.

**3**

# *MAKING CONNECTIONS*

Before we begin, pray a prayer like this:

*Father God, open my mind so that I may understand the Scriptures, and my eyes that I may behold wondrous things in Your Word.*

## *STEP FOUR: FIND A "KEY PHRASE."*

Look at Psalm 40 and find a phrase that "sticks to you" and seems to sum up the whole psalm. It needs to be a phrase that connects to various verses throughout the psalm. Once you find a phrase that you think is represented in several verses, draw a box around it, or highlight it, like this: key phrase. There is no right or wrong answer here.

Once you have found your key phrase, underline the words or phrases in different verses that relate to it. Draw an arrow from your key phrase to each underlined phrase or word.

## *STEP FIVE: GIVE YOUR STUDY A TITLE AND RECORD THE INSIGHTS YOU'VE GLEANED.*

Give this psalm a title based on what you've read and the observations you've made. Often the title may be the same as your key phrase.

Once you've given Psalm 40 a title, write down a few insights that you've gleaned in your study of the psalm. You may want to start with the phrase that you identified in Step Four.

**4**

# *INTERPRETATION AND APPLICATION*

Before we begin, pray a prayer like this:

*Father God, open my mind so that I may understand the Scriptures, and my eyes that I may behold wondrous things in Your Word.*

## *INTERPRETATION—WHERE CURIOSITY MEETS TRUTH*

When we interpret a Bible passage we are asking, *What does it mean?* In the interpretation stage, we finally get to answer some of the big questions we have. For example, in reading Psalm 40:1 you might have asked the question, *What do I do while I'm waiting for the Lord?* (We'll cover that question in Session Three.)

And now you might be asking, *How do I find the answers?* Great question.

## *HOW DO I FIND THE ANSWERS TO MY QUESTIONS?*

**ASK THE HOLY SPIRIT TO GUIDE YOU AND LEAD YOU INTO TRUTH.** Ask Him for humility, wisdom, revelation, and insight. Ask Him to guard you from your own agenda and to help you seek purity in your approach to His Word.

**USE CROSS-REFERENCES.** The first place to find your answers is in the pages of Scripture. Look for passages related to the passage that brought up your question. This process of using cross-references is known as Scripture interpreting Scripture. It's a wonderful way to be enlightened to the full context and connectedness of the Word. Before you head to a commentary, head right back to Scripture.

**LOOK AT VARIOUS TRANSLATIONS OF A PASSAGE.** I love BibleHub.com because it allows me to search for a verse or phrase and then see that verse or phrase in several different translations. If I'm stuck on something, I'll head to the Lexicon there to try and gain further understanding of a passage.

**USE COMMENTARIES!** Use these resources after you have studied on your own. You can find commentaries online for free. (Thank you, technology!) Make sure to read a wide variety of commentaries in order to get a full picture of what you are studying, always testing what you read against Scripture. You may want to reach out to your pastor or church staff for commentary recommendations.

It's also important to take into account biblical context, culture, history, genre, imagery, and language. The more you study the more you'll learn.

When you ask a question that brings up anger, fear, or deep sadness, don't push it away. Tell God how you feel. Ask Him to show you the truth. Ask Him to show you His heart and character, revealing beyond what you see. *Give it time.*

## *INTERPRETING PSALM 40 AS A WHOLE*

What do you think Psalm 40 is communicating as a whole?

Why do you think David wrote Psalm 40? What do you think he was trying to communicate to God and others through his prayer?

What might God want us to understand about Himself and His people through this psalm?

## *APPLICATION*

Application is where the Holy Spirit meets our willingness to obey. Our willing-ness to apply what we've learned in the power of, and submission to, the Holy Spirit in our lives is one of the most important parts of our Bible study. If we gain knowledge of the Scripture but aren't willing to let it affect our lives, we've done nothing but study in vain. If we've memorized Scripture and are now awesome at Bible trivia, but our hearts aren't tender to our Father God, we've missed the whole point, the whole heart of God and His redemptive calling. Knowledge is good, but without love, it's nothing. Love changes us and carries us all the way to the end and into the Father's arms.

Jesus said:

> If you love me, you will keep my commandments.

**JOHN 14:15**

## *CHOOSING TO REMEMBER WHAT GOD DOES*

I encourage you to memorize Psalm 40:1-3 over the course of this study. As you may know by now, verses 1-3 are an overview of the whole psalm and are a beautiful picture of the cycle of redemption that God invites us all into.

> [1] I waited patiently for the LORD;
> he inclined to me and heard my cry.
> [2] He drew me up from the pit of destruction,
> out of the miry bog,
> and set my feet upon a rock,
> making my steps secure.
> [3] He put a new song in my mouth,
> a song of praise to our God.
> Many will see and fear,
> and put their trust in the LORD.

**PSALM 40:1-3**

SESSION TWO:

# CRYING OUT

I waited patiently for the LORD;
he inclined to me and heard my cry.

**PSALM 40:1**

# GROUP GUIDE

## WARM THINGS UP

Begin with a few questions to start your conversation.

> Name a few insights that you gleaned from your study of Psalm 40 this past week.

> Share the key phrase and title that you identified for Psalm 40.

> Did a certain part of the psalm particularly resonate with you? Explain.

## WATCH

To view Session Two's teaching from Sarah Mae, download the optional video bundle at LifeWay.com/Psalm40.

## CREATE CONVERSATION

> If you feel comfortable, share a time when you have cried out to the Lord in the past. How did God respond?

> When you're walking through a hard time, do you find it easier to go to God with your struggles or to the people around you? Explain.

> Read Psalm 40:17 aloud together. What do you think David might have meant when he said that he was "poor and needy"? Do you think of yourself as poor and needy before God? Why or why not?

> Discuss the end of Psalm 40:17. Do you know God as your Helper and Deliverer? If so, how have you seen Him be a Helper and Deliverer in your life? If not, why do you struggle to see Him that way?

Close by praying for the women in your group to see God as their Helper and Deliverer, to cry out to Him for help, knowing that He loves them, hears them, and will meet them in their honesty.

# 1

# *CRYING OUT*

### … he inclined to me
### and heard my cry.
### PSALM 40:1b

Before we begin, pray a prayer like this:

*Father God, open my mind so that I may understand the Scriptures, and my eyes that I may behold wondrous things in Your Word.*

The word "cry," *shavah* in the Hebrew transliteration, means specifically a "cry for help."[1] God heard David's cry for help.

> **READ** Psalm 40:2,12,14, and write down some of the reasons why David cried out to God for help.

> Why do we cry out? What are some things that cause people to cry out for help?

> Why do you think people choose not to cry out? What fears might they have in crying out to the Lord for help?

For most of us, the entry point to prayer is a need for help. We know we can't fix or face our troubles alone. Even when we're scared, unsure, or we convince ourselves for a time that we can handle it, the truth is, God is our only hope. As the psalmist says in Psalm 73:25, "Whom have I in heaven but you?"

And yet, often, in a tucked away place in our souls, we find this thought: *If I cry out, I might get hurt.* To cry out for help is to be in a place of vulnerable risk. Or, as the psalmist teaches us, it's to be in a place of vulnerable trust.

Let's discuss two questions that I think hinder our surrendering to a vulnerable trust in God—one where we are free to cry out without fear or pretense:

1) Does God *really* hear my cries?
2) Can I *really* trust Him?

Do you struggle to surrender to God? If yes, which of the above questions best represents your struggle to come to God? Explain.

Now let's see what God has to say in answer to these questions.

## *DOES GOD HEAR MY CRIES?*

READ Psalm 34:15. Whose cry does God hear?

The Bible tells us because of Jesus' sacrifice on the cross, believers in Christ are counted righteous before God. We get credit for Jesus' righteousness in the eyes of God. (See Rom. 5:19; 2 Cor. 5:21; and Phil. 3:9.)

Does God hear your cries? How do you know?

## CAN I TRUST HIM?

Trust is a tender thing when we've been hurt or when we struggle with God's goodness based on our experiences and our perspectives. Before we look at the Scriptures, consider this prayer:

*Father, thank You that You know all the things I don't and that You understand everything that I can't. Please help me to see You, to trust You, and to be vulnerable with You. Thank You for Jesus. In His name I ask these things. Amen.*

Write your own prayer below:

**READ** Psalm 139:1-18. With how many of your ways is God acquainted?

Do you know what tomorrow will bring? Does God know?

God has packed the Bible full of beautiful, truthful promises to His children: He promises to be near to the brokenhearted (Ps. 34:18). He knows the distress of our souls (Ps. 31:7), and He promises never to forsake those who seek Him (Ps. 9:10). He cares about our pain. We even see Jesus crying with His followers here on earth (John 11:32-35).

**READ** Matthew 12:20. What do you think it means that God would not break a broken reed or quench a smoldering wick?

The entire Bible is the story of God's love for us, culminating in our rescue with the death and resurrection of Jesus and the outpouring of the Holy Spirit into each of us, sealing us (Eph. 1:13) for the day when all things will be made right and new (Rev. 21:5).

How do we know we can trust God? Because He proved He is trustworthy by showing the ultimate display of love for us. "Greater love has no one than this, that someone lay down his life for his friends" (John 15:13). If we believe God loves us, then we must believe that we can trust Him. His love took Him to the depths, and when we're in the depths, it is His love that preserves us (Ps. 40:11).

So how do we reconcile His love and trustworthiness to our fearful, sometimes arrogant ways of thinking, living, and feeling? We tell the truth.

## TELLING THE TRUTH: BEING HONEST WITH OUR PAIN AND PRAISE

Can you imagine singing Psalm 13:1 in church? "How long, O LORD? Will you forget me forever? How long will you hide your face from me?" It's honest though, right? Raw, real, recognizable? U2 singer Bono puts it bluntly when he says, "Why I'm suspicious of Christians is because of this lack of realism."[2] God is not afraid of our honesty.

READ Psalm 13:1. What did David ask the Lord?

READ Job 30:20-21. Whom was Job addressing?

God allows honest and vulnerable prayers and songs in a spirit of humility. He even shows us examples of saints of old addressing Him with accounts of their honest pain and confusion because of their limited human understanding.

The beauty of truth telling with each other and before God is that it clears the way for us to come out of hiding and into the light, where we see and acknowledge our pain and questions and confusion. When we do this, when we let the truth out, we are better able to ask God to help us heal. When we trust Him with our pain, we grow to know Him more as a loving Father who draws near to the brokenhearted, sits with us in our hurt and confusion, and leads us to gospel-anchored hope, joy, peace, and purpose. When we do this, when we let the truth out, we are better able to see the pain and questions and confusion of others and love them in it, not rushing their processes with God, just as God has been graciously patient with us in ours. To sing together with honest lyrics is to corporately sit with each other and agree that pain and praise are both threads that weave this tapestry of life.

How has God used today's time of study to speak to your heart and mind? How will you respond to Him?

## ②

# *CRYING OUT: OUR SIN*

<sup>12</sup> For evils have encompassed me
beyond number;
my iniquities have overtaken me,
and I cannot see;
they are more than the hairs of my head;
my heart fails me.
<sup>13</sup> Be pleased, O LORD, to deliver me!
O LORD, make haste to help me!

## PSALM 40:12-13

Before we begin, pray a prayer like this:

*Father God, open my mind so that I may understand the Scriptures, and my eyes that I may behold wondrous things in Your Word.*

Circle the words "evils" and "iniquities" in the above passage.

Here, the word "evils" has to do with trouble, distress, and misery. "Iniquities" describes our sin and the consequences our sin has on us and others. Both bring pain. These words have a similar meaning, and they share a common concept.

Circle other words or phrases in this passage that share a similar meaning or concept. What do you see?

David was focusing on one main idea in these verses. What was he trying to communicate?

Can you relate to David? Have you ever felt completely overwhelmed and overtaken by troubles? Have you ever felt the weight and regret and guilt of your sin or seen its consequences ripple out to others, causing them misery? Explain.

Rewrite this passage in your own words, communicating the same idea.

Let's take a closer look at the evils that surrounded David.

## THE EVILS THAT SURROUND DAVID

To understand just how all-encompassing the troubles were in David's life, we need to first understand a crucial part of his story: his anointing and his relationship with King Saul. I'm going to quickly summarize the highlights of David's story that we need to understand for our study. The rest of the story is fascinating; I encourage you to read it for yourself. If you'd like to read more, David's story is told in 1 Samuel 16–1 Kings 2:11.

For years, God set aside a group of people for Himself, to be His people, called the Israelites. God ruled them as their King. After many years, God's people asked God for an earthly king, so that they could be like the other nations around them.

Though their request did not please God, He gave them what they wanted and appointed Saul to be their king. Saul ruled as king for years, but the Lord eventually rejected him because of his failure to obey God (1 Sam. 13; 15).

In Saul's place, God chose David, a man after His own heart, to be the next king of Israel (1 Sam. 13:14). God sent the prophet Samuel to anoint David, but it would be several years before David would begin his reign. In fact, even though he had already been anointed as king, David would spend years in the service of Saul, fighting military battles for him and serving in his court. At several points during David's years of service, Saul became jealous of him—David quickly gained military notoriety and became more favored by the people than Saul. In fact, Saul became so jealous that he tried to kill David several times, forcing David to become a fugitive of sorts. David was constantly on the run, hiding in caves, traveling from place to place, unsure of who he could trust. It was a weary existence. He often cried out, lamenting to the Lord and begging for help. On at least two occasions, while on the run from Saul, David had the opportunity to kill the king, but he resisted out of respect for the Lord; Saul was still technically God's anointed king for that time (1 Sam. 24; 26). David hadn't been given the throne yet. David remained faithful and steadfast in God, trusting Him completely.

Saul was a complicated man, tortured by his own jealousy and pride, and yet he possessed a small softness of heart. He was able to feel the Lord's conviction (1 Sam. 15:24-25), but his conviction never led him to true repentance.

> Take a moment right now to think if there's anything that God has convicted you of that you need to repent of, and if there is, repent of it (let God know you want to turn from this sin). Write a prayer of repentance here. Remember, repentance is a continuous process, so your walking in light may be a gradual change and you may have to walk away from this sin more than once.

When Saul died in battle, David lamented over him. Shortly after, David was appointed king of Judah, and eventually, king of Israel.

## HOW GREAT THE SIN OF THE MAN
## AFTER GOD'S OWN HEART

In large part, the Bible portrays David as faithful and upright, demonstrating his full confidence in and fear of the Lord. But, David wasn't perfect. Let's take a look at an instance of sin in his life.

**READ** 2 Samuel 11. Look closely at verses 1-5. What was David's problem?

David tried to cover up his sin in several ways. List them below.

How often do we, like David, in trying to fix or cover up our sin, just go deeper into more sin? William Paul Young says that getting caught "is a great and terrifying grace."[3] David received that grace from his friend and prophet, Nathan.

**READ** 2 Samuel 12:1-25. How did God respond to David's sin—in sending Nathan to confront David? In the consequences of David's sin? In His response to David's repentance?

How did David respond to being rebuked? Note especially against whom David says he sinned. (If you have time, read Psalm 51, a psalm David wrote after Nathan confronted him.)

## WHAT ABOUT OUR SIN?

Why do we so often stay in the darkness of our sin, struggling to confess our sins to God and godly community?

You know that gross feeling you get when you know you're in sin or you haven't confessed a hidden sin from your past? It's a slimy feeling in your gut that no matter how hard you try, you can't get rid of. It's always there, just under the surface of your skin, keeping you from feeling pure, from having a clear conscience. It's a severe mercy of God called conviction of sin. While it may be uncomfortable at times, conviction of sin is a kindness of the Holy Spirit—leading us back to God in repentance and faith, reminding us that God is not finished with us yet. He has plans for our future, and they are good. There is only one way to get rid of that feeling, of that grossness: confession.

**READ** 1 John 1:8-9. What are we told to do in order to be forgiven? What will God do if we confess?

The Greek word for confess in verse 9 is *homologeo,* and it means "to declare openly,"[4] acknowledging and agreeing with God that what you are doing or what you did was wrong. God says if we confess our sins and turn from them, He'll forgive us and bring us back into right relationship with Him. We confess in order to be right with God.

Sometimes God also tells us to confess to one another.

**READ** James 5:13-16. Why do we confess to one another?

When we confess before the Lord, whom our sins are always primarily against, He forgives us and cleanses us. When we confess to one another, we are healed. And that word "healed" carries a meaning of being made whole. How? How does confessing to someone cause healing and wholeness? This passage in James refers to the power of intercessory prayer in accountability as we love one another enough to fight for the holiness of our brothers and sisters and the intimacy of their relationships with Christ. As scholar Ralph P. Martin says, "The author [of this passage] is showing that the prayer, not the person, ... is the channel through which God's power to heal is conveyed."[5] In confession of sin to one another, we bring our brothers and sisters before God in prayer, asking Him to heal them.

The grossness *only* goes away when we confess and choose to walk in the light, no matter how scary, no matter the consequences. Nothing, no hidden sin or fear of exposure or awful outcome, is worth compromising the freedom you have when your conscience is clear and your heart is pure before the Lord.

What can you learn from David's example of repentance?

How has God used today's time of study to speak to your heart and mind? How will you respond to Him?

## 3

# *CRYING OUT: OUR ENEMIES*

¹⁴ Let those be put to shame and disappointed
altogether who seek to snatch away my life;
let those be turned back and brought to dishonor
who delight in my hurt!
¹⁵ Let those be appalled because of their shame
who say to me, "Aha, Aha!"

**PSALM 40:14-15**

Before we begin, pray a prayer like this:

*Father God, open my mind so that I may understand the Scriptures, and my eyes that I may behold wondrous things in Your Word.*

When you think of an enemy, who or what do you think of?

An enemy can be someone we don't even know (a terrorist, for example), or he or she can be under our own roofs. An enemy can be a parent, a neighbor, or someone we work with. If we have a personal enemy, it's likely he or she has hurt us in a deep way, and we are valid in our feelings of caution. Anger is honest. If someone hurts my child, I might feel anger or disdain toward that person. If someone abused me, I might feel anger toward him or her.

David understood these honest feelings and went so far as to ask God to harm or humiliate his enemies. Please don't misunderstand, it's not that these declarations of harm should be carried out, or that God is OK with our vengeance. Rather, God wants us to pray honestly and to bring these honest feelings to Him so that they no longer consume us.

Look at Psalm 40:14-15 and list the things David wants for his enemies.

If you have an enemy, go ahead and write the truth about what you'd like to happen to that person in the margin. This is practice in getting out the truth of how you really feel. (God knows it all anyway.)

OK, now take a deep breath and thank God that He allows the truth of our pain to be acknowledged; no hiding, no pretense.

Let's go to the Scriptures to see what we can learn about our enemies.

READ John 10:10; Ephesians 6:12; and 1 Peter 5:8-9. Who is our chief enemy, the one who deceives man and causes pain, destruction, and evil influences? Who is our battle *not* with?

READ James 4:7. What's our first line of defense in dealing with Satan?

We wrestle with our chief enemy, Satan, along with "the spiritual forces of evil in the heavenly places" (Eph. 6:12) and with our own flesh and fallen nature. I don't have to tell you that we also daily deal with people around us who can act like enemies.

READ Matthew 5:43-48. How does Jesus tell us to treat our enemies?

READ Romans 12:17-21. Instead of repaying the evil done to us or taking revenge, what does God instruct us to do?

As The Jewish Encyclopedia notes, "Kindness bestowed upon an enemy is called 'heaping coals of fire upon his head,' since it tends to waken his deadened conscience and help him to realize his wrong."[6] God uses grace and kindness to lead us to repentance (Rom. 2:4). We're to do the same with others.

Think of a recent conflict you've experienced. If you're honest, how did your attitudes and actions line up with what God teaches us in Matthew 5 and Romans 12? Explain.

If you have room for growth in this area, and I think we all do, list one or two tangible ways you might have handled the situation described above differently, to infuse more grace and kindness into the encounter.

Loving our enemies is impossible for us to do on our own. We need God to empower us to do it. And, let's be honest, it sometimes makes no sense to us. Why would God possibly ask us to love the people who hurt us the most? Who wants to love the person who causes us trouble at work, the person who hurt our child, or the person who has violated us? Who wants to love the abusive father, the alcoholic mother, the bully, or the terrorist? What is God thinking?

Why do you think God calls us to love our enemies? Jot down any thoughts below.

Remember what we read in Matthew 5:43-48? When we love our enemies, we are acting like our Father in heaven who not only tells the sun to rise and the rain to fall on the just and the unjust alike, but who reached out to us and made us His children when we were His enemies (Rom. 5:10). The Matthew 5 passage shows us that God uses loving our enemies as a way to make us look more like Him, chipping away our earthiness to create more of His character in us. It's God's blessing—working even the hard things for the good of His children.

Think back to David and Saul, and how David had the opportunity to kill Saul, free and clear. In those moments, in those choices David made not to kill Saul, he loved him. He loved his enemy (remember, love is an action) because he trusted God, and it broke Saul's heart because he saw that David was more righteous than he. Saul had every opportunity to turn from his evil ways, but he chose to let his selfish ambition lead him. David trusted the outcome to the Lord. And there it is: Trust. Do we trust the Lord to deal with our enemies? Do we believe God will use these hard circumstances for our good? Or do we believe it's solely up to us to make things OK?

Journal your thoughts to God. If you struggle to trust Him with your enemies, tell Him about it. If you gladly submit your hard relationships to God, praise Him for His grace and care for you.

## DO I HAVE TO MAINTAIN A RELATIONSHIP WITH SOMEONE WHO HAS DONE EVIL TO ME OR TO SOMEONE I LOVE?

I want to be very careful here. Loving our enemies does not mean we are to stay in abusive or harmful situations. You are free in Christ to use wisdom and set boundaries that protect you and your family. You've been given authorities to deal with wrongdoers, and you do not have to associate with someone who is doing evil in this manner (Prov. 4:14-15; 1 Cor. 5:11). The key is to be sensitive to the Holy Spirit, be consistent in your study of God's Word and participation in godly community, and be willing to do whatever God asks of you, so you have a clear conscience before Him.

As to forgiveness of enemies, there is so much freedom in choosing to forgive. See the appendix on page 182 for "6 Ways to Forgive." I love what Henry Cloud and John Townsend say in their book, *Boundaries*:

> Forgiveness gives me boundaries because it unhooks me from the hurtful person, and then I can act responsibly, wisely. If I am not forgiving them, I am still in a destructive relationship with them.[7]

God works mightily when we forgive. Reach out to friends or godly church leaders if you're in a troubling situation or relationship and you aren't sure what to do. The Lord is with you. We've been asking ourselves some tough emotional and spiritual questions. If you think you may need more support than your group can offer, reach out to your pastor or a trained Christian counselor. God has given us so many resources to use to walk in health and joy. Let's receive those gifts.

How did God speak to your heart and mind in this session?

Considering what we've studied, is there anyone you need to forgive?

**(4)**

# *CRYING OUT: OUR POOR AND NEEDY STATE*

## As for me, I am poor and needy, but the Lord takes thought for me.
### PSALM 40:17a

Before we begin, pray a prayer like this:

*Father God, open my mind so that I may understand the Scriptures, and my eyes that I may behold wondrous things in Your Word.*

> **READ** Genesis 2:7 and Job 34:14-15. Where did your breath come from?

It's not something we often consider or discuss. But we, each and every one of us, are breathing because God is sustaining us. Every breath, every heartbeat, He is holding our lives in His hands, just as He holds the universe together (Col. 1:17). If God decided to gather His breath back to Himself, Job 34:15 tells us that "all flesh would perish together, and man would return to dust." Our physical existence, no matter how self-sufficient we feel on a daily basis, depends utterly and entirely on God. But, what about our spiritual state?

**READ** Ephesians 2:1-9, and complete the blanks below.
Without Jesus, we are:


With Jesus, we are:


Do we have in ourselves the ability to be alive? How are we made alive?


**READ** John 15:5. What can we do apart from Jesus?


All of us are poor and needy and are always at the mercy of God, whether we believe in Him or not, whether we trust Him or not. Our very breath is a mercy. We are therefore physically and spiritually poor and in need of Jesus every single day. We are all dependent on Him from the minute our lungs take in that first gasp of breath to the moment that breath leaves us. And again, whose breath is in our lungs? The very breath of God. In fact, every time you breathe you are quite possibly saying His name, because scholars believe His very name is the sound of our breath: YHWH.

"… scholars have noted that the letters YHWH represent breathing sounds, aspirated consonants that in the Hebrew alphabet would be transliterated like this:

Yod, rhymes with "rode," which we transliterate "Y"
He, rhymes with "say," which we transliterate "H"
Vav, like "lava," which we transliterate "V" or "W"
He, rhymes with "say," which we transliterate "H"

A wonderful question rises to excite the imagination: what if the name of God is the sound of breathing?"[8]

The first thing we do as a newborn is inhale the breath
of life that is God's Name, and the last thing we do,
in the moment of our death, is exhale that Name.[9]

**JAMES DAVID AUDLIN**

When you really think about your true physical and spiritual reality before God, how do you feel? Comforted? Anxious? Explain.

Acknowledging our need before God and our true dependence on Him can be a little unnerving, but I'm here to tell you it's a great thing.

## *THE VERY GOOD NEWS IN BEING POOR AND NEEDY*

**READ** Matthew 5:3. What word did Jesus use to describe the poor in spirit? What is theirs?

I love the ESV Study Bible's commentary on this Matthew passage. It says, "The poor in spirit are those who recognize they are in need of God's help." The kingdom of God "belongs to those who confess their spiritual bankruptcy."[10] The Greek word for "poor" here, *ptochos*, means to be as helpless as a beggar. The Hebrew words used in Psalm 40:17 for "poor" and "needy" are *ani* and *ebyon*. They convey the same meaning: "destitute – beggar, needy."[11] Why do you think Jesus would say that someone who is as helpless as a beggar is blessed and that theirs is the kingdom of heaven? I think it's because God's redemptive grace bridges the chasm between our sin and His righteousness—turning God's enemy into His friend, the lost into the found, and the beggar into the blessed (2 Cor. 12:9-11).

## *WHAT DOES IT MEAN TO BE BLESSED?*

When you hear the word *blessed* what comes into your mind?

The word *blessing*, as in God blessing His people and His people blessing Him with praise, in the Greek (*eulogeo*) means to grant or bestow what is beneficial, what will result in good. Oddly enough, it's the word translated as "bless" in the KJV translation of Matthew 5:44: "Love your enemies, bless them that curse you." When you think of blessing, think of Romans 8:28, how God is working all things together for our good.

READ Ephesians 1:3-14. Focus on verse 3. What are Christians, those who recognize their poor and needy state, blessed with?

List below all of the spiritual blessings God gives His children, as described in the Ephesians passage.

READ these Scriptures and list other ways a person is blessed.

Matthew 5:1-11

Luke 11:28

Romans 4:7

James 1:2-4

Pick one of the blessings or ways that we've been blessed by God that we've discussed above and ask God to help you understand it more. Write the blessing you've chosen to study further below.

We're blessed with God's Spirit to help us when we are poor and needy, when we humbly acknowledge the truth that we are utterly dependent on God for our lives and our spiritual conditions. It's in this humility and understanding that we can have the confidence to cry out to God for help, knowing that He takes thought of us. What a comfort. What grace.

How did God speak to your heart and mind today? How will you respond to Him?

SESSION THREE:

# WAITING

I waited patiently for the LORD;
he inclined to me and heard my cry.

**PSALM 40:1**

# GROUP GUIDE

## WARM THINGS UP

Here are a few questions to begin your time.

> What from your personal study this past week was really impactful for you?
>
> Think about a time recently you've had to deal with an enemy in your life. Why is it difficult to apply the gospel message of loving our enemies?
>
> What do you feel when you think about your true state before God? Explain.

## WATCH

To view Session Three's teaching from Sarah Mae, download the optional video bundle at LifeWay.com/Psalm40.

## CREATE CONVERSATION

> What do you hate waiting for? Feel free to share everyday things, like waiting in traffic, or something more serious.
>
> Why do you think God sometimes makes us wait for Him in things we want or think we need?
>
> Can you think of a time God made you wait, only to let you later see His faithfulness? Explain.
>
> In what area of your life do you most struggle with trusting God? Explain.

Close your time with prayer, asking God to help you desire His face more than His hand, and His presence more than His blessings. Ask Him to remind you that He is faithful in seasons of waiting.

Optional video sessions available for purchase at LifeWay.com/Psalm40

_____

_____

_____

_____

_____

_____

_____

_____

_____

_____

_____

_____

_____

_____

_____

_____

_____

_____

_____

_____

_____

_____

_____

_____

_____

# *BOUND UP WITH GOD*

## I waited patiently for the LORD ...
### PSALM 40:1

Before we begin, pray a prayer like this:

*Father God, open my mind so that I may understand the Scriptures, and my eyes that I may behold wondrous things in Your Word.*

### *WHAT ARE YOU WAITING FOR?*

Some of us are waiting for a husband.
Some of us are waiting for a child.
Some of us are waiting for healing.
Some of us are waiting for justice.
Some of us are waiting for a callback.
Some of us are waiting for what our next steps should be.
Some of us are waiting for relief.
Some of us are waiting for our child to return to God.
Some of us are waiting for escape.
Some of us are waiting for those we love to come to know the Lord.

What are you waiting for? What unanswered prayer continues to leave your lips? What impossible prayer have you almost given up praying?

In the above verse, circle the phrase "waited patiently."

In the Hebrew, "waited patiently" is stated *qavah qavah*. The same Hebrew word is used for both "waited" and "patiently" in our English Bible. The word *qavah* means "to wait, look for, hope, expect."[1] It's almost as if David was saying, "I waited and waited with eager eyes." It's interesting to note that the root of the word, the literal translation, means to "bind together," giving the image of weaving or twisting together into something like a rope.

**READ** the following Scriptures, which I've emphasized for clarity.

And God said, "Let the waters under the heavens be gathered together [*qavah*] into one place, and let the dry land appear." And it was so.

### GENESIS 1:9

Indeed, none who wait [*qavah*] for you shall be put to shame; they shall be ashamed who are wantonly treacherous.

### PSALM 25:3

Let's try something as an exercise. What if instead of using the word *wait* in each of these passages, you used the words *bound up*?

Let the waters in the heavens be *bound up* together.

None who are *bound up* with you shall be put to shame.

I can't help but wonder if the original audience of the Bible would have carried together both understandings of the word *qavah* in what the author was communicating. What if David was saying that because he was bound, intimately and intricately, with the Lord, that even in the pain of waiting and waiting, there is hope? Remember, the word *qavah* isn't just waiting—it's waiting and looking and hoping and expecting. This kind of waiting is done by someone who knows the Lord is trustworthy.

**READ** Psalm 22:9. How are we, and all of humanity, bound to God from birth?

## *BOUND UP WITH CHRIST*

**READ** Ephesians 1:13. What happens when you believe (entrust yourself) in Jesus?

**READ** 1 Corinthians 6:17. What happens when you unite, or bind, yourself with Christ?

We are *all* bound to God in our humanity; every single person on this earth is dependent on Him from birth. (Remember our breath?) When we recognize our needy state before God and we entrust ourselves to Jesus, we become bound up with Him through the Holy Spirit. We trust Him with our humanity and our souls and for our eternities.

There is also something to be said in binding ourselves to God in an active, mindful, *settling*. We can choose to settle it within ourselves that God is good, how He acts is always for our good, and what He says is true, whether we understand it or not. In this settling we're saying, "I've thrown in my lot with you, GOD, and I'm not budging" (Ps. 26:1, The Message).

Once we've bound ourselves to God, we join the company of David, with no masks or fake religiosity, just honest feelings and prayers in the midst of embracing the truth of His goodness and our belonging to God as His children.

## *BOUND UP WITH AND WAITING FOR GOD*

Think back to Psalm 40:1. David was waiting *for* the Lord. Scripture is full of instruction to wait on God and examples of heroes of the faith who've done just that. If you have time, I recommend reading Psalm 38:15; 39:7; and 130:5 to see a few encouraging examples.

What do you think it means to wait for the Lord?

Is there a circumstance in your life in which you're waiting on the Lord? If yes, describe it below.

**READ** Psalm 121:1-2 and Micah 7:7. In our waiting, where does God tell us to set the eyes of our hearts? Where does our help come from?

Waiting for the Lord is the key in all the waiting, because it is not dependent on the circumstance but rather on Him and what He's doing in, through, and around us for good.

My mom was a sun-up, sun-down, vodka-drinking alcoholic for twenty years. I begged God to save her, to make her stop drinking, to do *something* because I hated her, but I knew God called me to love her. Our relationship was strained and tense, heartbreaking and manipulative. For years I prayed. Even after I had all but given up hope, I prayed. Then one day I got a call from a hospital worker telling me that my mom wasn't going to live long.

"Mom, what happened?" I said. "How did you end up in the hospital?"

"Well," my mom said. "I'm here because God told me to stop drinking."

Through more than ten years of praying for my mom, I learned that the Lord was most interested in my heart. He drew me close to Him in trust until my hope was no longer in the outcome of my prayer, but in Him alone. When the miracle (and it was a miracle) did occur, it was a blessed surprise—shocking, really—and worthy of praise and exaltation! My heart was in utter gratitude. But the answer to my prayer, as awesome (in the truest sense of the word) as it was, wasn't the hope of my life as it had once been. I had mourned my mom, lamenting the loss of a mother, and given her into God's loving hands.[2] I never stopped praying, but my peace was in the Lord. Having that peace allowed me to keep going and to find joy in life despite the heartache.

When we wait for the Lord, we cry out and we ask Him to make a way, to fix it, to do something else. We fall to our knees, faces to the ground, and we beg Him to answer our prayers. And then we say, as Jesus did in Mark 14:36, in full assurance of God's divine knowledge and goodness, "not what I will, but what you will." Submitting to God's will can be difficult, especially because we can't see the full picture that God sees.

> Think back to the circumstances you described on page 61—the one you're waiting on the Lord to answer. Journal an honest prayer about your waiting below. Tell Him the sad and happy things you're feeling. Close your prayer by acknowledging the truth of God's Word and His goodness, even though you can't see it now.

If it feels sometimes like God is being cruel in your waiting, my prayer for you is that the following passage would be the meditation of your heart. God wants your hope to be in Him, apart from any outcome or circumstance. Call out to Him in prayer. He promises to be near.

<sup>17</sup> The LORD is righteous in all his ways

and kind in all his works.

<sup>18</sup> The LORD is near to all who call on him,

to all who call on him in truth.

**PSALM 145:17-18**

**2**

# *WHEN TEARS BLUR OUR VISION*

Blessed is the man who makes
the LORD his trust,
who does not turn to the proud,
to those who go astray after a lie!

**PSALM 40:4**

Before we begin, pray a prayer like this:

*Father God, open my mind so that I may understand the Scriptures, and my eyes that I may behold wondrous things in Your Word.*

**READ** Psalm 6:6. What was David weary with?

Have you ever been so sad that your bed seemed flooded with your tears? I have. I can remember times of crying so hard I thought my head would explode. This kind of weeping, the intensity of the heartache, wears you out, body and soul. These kinds of tears make it hard to see; everything becomes a blur. Even if you're not much of a crier, we've all known grief, heartache, and pain in some form. This pain often skews the way we see the world. A blurred perspective can lead to depression, pride, anger, and turning away from God.

**READ** Psalm 40:4, and fill in the blanks.

Blessed is the man who _____,

who does not _____.

## TURNING TO THE PROUD AND GOING ASTRAY AFTER A LIE

The Hebrew word used for "proud" in Psalm 40:4 is the same word *Rahab* (not the person), used by the God to symbolically refer to Egypt in Isaiah 30:1-7.[3] The word literally means *storm* and carries a figurative meaning of arrogance.

**READ** Isaiah 30:1-7. Where are God's people seeking their refuge?


What two words did God use to describe Egypt's help? What did God call Egypt in verse 7?


So full were Egyptian politics of bluster and big language, that the Hebrews had a nickname for Egypt. They called her Rahab—*Stormy speech, Blusterer, Braggart.* It was the term also for the crocodile, as being a *monster*, so that there was a picturesqueness as well as moral aptness in the name. Ay, says Isaiah, catching at the old name and putting to it another which describes Egyptian helplessness and inactivity, I call her *Rahab Sit-still, Braggart-that-sitteth-still, Stormy-speech Stay-at-home. Blustering and inactivity, blustering and sitting still,* that is her character. *For Egypt helpeth in vain and to no purpose.*[4]

**PROFESSOR G. A. SMITH, D. D.**

In this Isaiah passage, God's people bought into the lie that Egypt, the seemingly impressive political superpower, would help and protect them. They ignored God's promise of provision and instead sought to meet their own needs in a way that made sense to men. They circumvented the need to wait on God.

When we turn to the proud or go astray after a lie, we're turning to what may look good, but in reality, is worthless and empty. We may be angry. We may doubt God's goodness. We may be walking through deep pain. We may simply be tired of waiting. Whatever the case, God wants us to take refuge in Him alone because He offers fruitfulness (good out of our pain) and fullness (joy in the midst of our pain).

What does turning to the proud or going astray after a lie have to do with weeping and waiting? Have you ever known anyone who has grown bitter or resentful in his or her pain? If we're not careful, pain has a way of hardening our hearts. How about someone whose pain seemed to cause him or her to give up or escape into the temporary comfort of social media, mindless entertainment, excessive sleeping, binge shopping, drugs, alcohol, or some other addiction? (Yes, even Christians.) Sometimes in our pain and in the waiting we begin to look elsewhere for our help. With blurred vision, the ideas of the world can become appealing. Or we may be angry with God, and we no longer believe His goodness. When we don't feel God's presence in our pain and in the wait, it's tempting to go where we find what seems like relief.

Have you ever looked to the world's ways to find relief? If so, how? How did that end up for you?

Has there ever been a time in your life when your heart was hardened toward God? If so, what were the circumstances?

Take a moment to consider your answers to the two preceding questions. Why do you think you sought relief in the world or hardened your heart toward God? Do you see any common reasons between the two?

When we're seeking comfort instead of turning to the Lord, sometimes we turn away from Him and seek out things of the flesh to fill the gap or mask the hurt. Paul mentioned some of these things in Galatians 5:17-21.

READ Galatians 5:17-21, and list below the works of the flesh mentioned in the passage.

Feel free to take a few minutes to research any of the terms from the list of "the works of the flesh" (v. 19) that you don't understand. In verse 21, where it says, "those who do such things" the passage means those who "practice such things." The word for "practice" in the Greek is *prasso* and implies to keep doing something repeatedly, in other words, actively choosing to stay in sin.[5] The idea here is that there has been no turning, no repenting of whatever sins we gravitate toward. It's those people who will not inherit the kingdom. As Christians, we will struggle with sin (see Rom. 7:15-20 and Paul's relatable description of doing what he doesn't want to do, and vice versa), but that is different than choosing to ignore the truth and stay in our sin. We must be quick to repent or walk away from sins, especially staying on guard for those sins we naturally gravitate toward.

READ Psalm 16:4, and write the first half of the verse below.

What ultimately happens when we turn to something other than God for help?

The world and its desires can only offer us a false fix.

## *MAKING THE LORD OUR TRUST*

**READ** Psalm 57:2. What did David say God does?

**READ** Philippians 1:6. What will God bring to completion?

Consider the promises of Psalm 57:2 and Philippians 1:6 together. Do you struggle to believe that God will fulfill His purposes for you and complete His work in you? Explain.

When we're stumbling with blurred vision, when our anger and pain and confusion are overwhelming, and the wait is long and His presence seems far away, what do we do?

**READ** 2 Corinthians 5:7.

We don't rely on our sight, but by faith, we trust and believe God is who He says He is, even when it's just so hard.

Think of an area of struggle or uncertainty in your life today. (Maybe it's the circumstance you mentioned yesterday—the one in which you're waiting on the Lord.) What would it look like for you to walk practically by faith, not sight, in that circumstance? Pray for God to help you do it. Use the space below to journal.

God understands this pain; He knows we need to express our feelings and pain in an honest way. And that honest way? It's called lament. In the next session, we're going to talk about lament—what it means and how to do it.

**（３）**

# *LAMENT*

## … my heart fails me.
### PSALM 40:12b

Before we begin, pray a prayer like this:

*Father God, open my mind so that I may understand the Scriptures, and my eyes that I may behold wondrous things in Your Word.*

When there's nothing else to do, when the pain is too much, when prayers don't get answered the way we had hoped, we lament.

More than one-third of the Book of Psalms are psalms of lament—raw, honest emotions with no pretense. *Strong's Exhaustive Concordance* defines *lament* as, "to tear the hair and beat the breasts."[6] Lament was not something to be hidden or ashamed of. When we lament, we allow space for the expression of deep, guttural pain.

In the Scriptures, we see people lamenting in a very specific way in order to express their grief.

> **READ** the following verses, and write down the expressions of lament in each.
>
> Esther 4:1-3
>
> Lamentations 2:10
>
> Daniel 9:3

## WHY ASHES?

Scholars aren't sure of the exact origin of the mourning ritual—why sackcloth and ashes were chosen in particular. However, we do have some ideas as to what these acts and items might have symbolized to mourners in the ancient Near East. To discuss this topic, we need to go back to the beginning.

> **READ** Genesis 3:19 and Genesis 18:27. What are we? Where will our bodies return?

In Genesis 3, we find God's address to Adam and Eve after the fall of humanity. In Genesis 18, we read the story of Abraham interceding on behalf of the people of Sodom and Gomorrah, cities of great evil that were due for God's judgment. In both instances, we find insights into humanity's low and humble state—God teaching us how our bodies would now be fallible because of the fall and return to dust, and Abraham's honest confession of humility as he dared to speak on behalf of the wicked before our holy God.

In the Old Testament, God gives His people the sacrificial system as a way to deal with their sin so that they can be right with God. Otherwise, as sinful people, the Old Testament Israelites would have only been at odds with God. You may know, the sacrificial system was not able to save people. Only faith in Christ's sacrifice and righteousness for us can do that. But, the sacrificial system foreshadowed Christ's sacrifice on the cross and our need for a Savior, a sacrifice that would nullify our need for this former temporary sacrificial system.

> **READ** Exodus 27:1-3, a passage that describes a part of the Old Testament sacrifice, the bronze altar. Why is a pot needed for this altar? What will it receive?

The bronze altar was the altar on which sacrifices were made. A burnt offering was an offering made through fire. The Hebrew word for "burnt" is *alah*, which means "to go up, ascend."[7] The offering laid on the fire produced a smoke, "a pleasing aroma" (Lev. 8:28), that went up to the Lord.

When the flesh of the sacrifice was burned, it became ashes, dust—like the dust of the ground from which God created Adam.

In Joshua 7:6, we read the first biblical account of dust being used in lament. Joshua and the elders were grieving because Israel had been defeated in battle, even after they had seen God's grace and provision in helping them successfully cross the Jordan and take the city of Jericho.

**READ** Joshua 6:18 and 7:1. Why did the Israelites suffer defeat?

The people didn't listen to God's command. They broke faith and took what wasn't theirs to take, just as Adam and Eve broke faith and took what wasn't theirs to take. It all goes back to the garden.

Dust to dust.

Ashes remind us not only of what we are but also of when it all went wrong, when the source of sorrow and heartache entered our world and how God is helping us make it right.

## WHY SACKCLOTH?

SACKCLOTH. A coarse cloth (Heb. *saq*, Gk. *sakkos*, from which the Eng. word is derived), usually made of goats' hair (Siphra 53b) and black in colour (Rev. 6:12).[8]

To understand the history of sackcloth in the Hebrew tradition, we need to take some time in the story of two of the patriarchs.

**READ** Genesis 27:5-40. Who deceived Isaac, and how did he do it?

What's the only way to get the skin of the goat—what must happen to the animal?

What's sackcloth made from again?

**READ** Genesis 37:12-35 (the first mention of sackcloth in the Scriptures). Why did Jacob lament? How did Jacob's sons deceive their father (v. 31)?

What did Jacob put on to show his grief (v. 34)?

The first mention of someone in the Bible wearing goat's hair is when Jacob used it to deceive his father, to take something that wasn't his to take (his brother's blessing). Jacob broke faith with his father. The first mention of someone wearing sackcloth, goat's hair, in the Bible is Jacob. His sons broke faith with him through deceit, taking something from him that wasn't theirs to take (their brother).

Sackcloth is a reminder of what isn't supposed to be. It reminds us of sin and the pain it brings. Sackcloth is " an outward sign of one's inward condition,"[9] a sign of humility and repentance before God.

## *LAMENT AND ITS UNDERCURRENT OF HOPE*

We acknowledge the very wrong things in this world, the things that we can't understand, things too painful to wrap our minds around. Lament allows us to sit in our grief for a while and let the truth of the pain be what it is. Because it hurts.

Don't rush those last two sentences.

As I'm writing this, I'm reminded of three very wrong things that have happened in the last three days: An eight car pile-up in my hometown in front of our high school just as school was letting out. Two students killed. For what? No sense in it. Just utter heartbreak. Yesterday a lovely young girl, only eighteen years old, was so haunted by her depression that she took her own life. And just this morning on the news, a shooting in a synagogue in my home state took eight souls from this earth. These devastating events are but a drop in the bucket of the pain experienced in this world every day, every minute.

We cry out, *Why Lord?* We just cry. Yes, we can do things to help our world, our communities, our friends, and as kingdom bringers and light bearers, we should. But our control is limited. Sin is still present, there's still darkness in the world, the behind-the-scenes spiritual battle still rages, and the enemy is still diligently working to destroy everything good.

Lament becomes our lifeline, tethering us to the reminder that while the pain in this world is brutal, worthy of tears, and "beating of the breast," our hope is bigger than the pain. At the table of the Lord before us there is always joy, victory, beauty, goodness, and peace to take hold of.

Most importantly, there is resurrection (life out of what was once dead) and redemption (deliverance into freedom).

READ Revelation 21:1-5; record the final verse of the passage below.

In Christ, there is no death. All of us who hope in Him will experience that glorious day when all will be made new. Relationships won't be broken. Drunk drivers and terrorists won't exist. Babies won't go to heaven too soon, and abuse will never, ever happen.

Until then, we wait, we remember, we take hold of the blessings we have in Christ, and we work to bring God's new life and redemption to the world, pushing back the darkness. Yes, it will all be made new one day, but even now God is redeeming hearts and minds, working in ways we cannot see.

Hope now and hope eternal. But always, there is hope.

**4**

# *REMEMBER*

² He drew me up from the pit of destruction …
³ He put a new song in my mouth …

## PSALM 40:2-3

Before we begin, pray a prayer like this:

*Father God, open my mind so that I may understand the Scriptures, and my eyes that I may behold wondrous things in Your Word.*

**READ** Psalm 63:5-8, and record below anything that stands out to you.

Looking at the Christian Standard Bible or English Standard Version translations of the Bible, write the first word in verse 6:

We must create occasions to remember the faithfulness of our God. Take a few minutes and ponder some of the specific things God has done for you. Write them down.

# A TIME LINE OF MY LIFE

☐ At the beginning of the line, draw a point and write your birth date. Feel free to be creative in how you fill in your time line. Make it your own.

☐ At the end of the line, draw a point and write onward. You don't know this date yet. It's when you will head onward into the presence of the Lord. Everything in between your birth date and your death date is your life.

☐ Take a few moments to write down points in your life that have been significant. Make sure to include when you gave your life to Jesus.

☐ Add points and, if possible, dates along with descriptions of what God has done for you. Include times when you've seen God work through your life.

How did God speak to you today?

What's your response to Him?

Write a psalm like the one David wrote in Psalm 63:5-8. Tell of what God has done, using actual events from your time line. You may want to include things that you know and love about God's character—anything that will help you remember who He is. Add a portion of the psalm that describes how you will praise Him, even in the dark when you can't see the light.

SESSION FOUR:

# GOD INCLINES TO US

He inclined to me and
heard my cry.

**PSALM 40:1b**

# GROUP GUIDE

## WARM THINGS UP

Here are a few questions to begin your time.

> Sarah Mae says, "Waiting for the Lord is the key in all the waiting, because it is not dependent on the circumstance but rather on Him and what He's doing in, through, and around us for good." Discuss this quote in your time together. Why is this difficult sometimes?
>
> What does it mean to you to lament?
>
> Does anyone want to share a piece of the psalm they composed or maybe their time line from Day 5's study?

## WATCH

To view Session Four's teaching from Sarah Mae, download the optional video bundle at LifeWay.com/Psalm40.

## CREATE CONVERSATION

> What does it mean to you to really see another person or be seen by another person?
>
> Read Genesis 16:13. Share a time when you know that the Lord looked after you. Explain the circumstance.
>
> What would you say to a friend who trusts God, but doesn't see Him working in her life as she might want Him to? Does His seeming inactivity mean He doesn't know what she's going through?

Close your time with prayer, asking God to show your group His faithfulness to see and care for each of you. Ask Him to show you people around you who may need to be seen and cared for by you this week.

# *HE SEES US*

## He inclined to me and heard my cry.
### PSALM 40:1b

Before we begin, pray a prayer like this:

*Father God, open my mind so that I may understand the Scriptures, and my eyes that I may behold wondrous things in Your Word.*

We know from Session One that God hears us. In this week's study we're going to learn what the Scriptures say about God seeing us. But first, let's look at the word *incline*.

If her child is hurt or sad, what's a good mother's first impulse to do?

**READ** the following Scriptures, and beside each reference, record the parent/child imagery you find in each.

Isaiah 49:15

Isaiah 66:13

John 1:12

Galatians 4:6

God is very specific with His language in Scripture. He very intentionally gives us the imagery of Him as our parent—our *Abba*, Father. It is purposeful that He gives us an image of Himself as our parent, our Father, and also as a comforting mother who could never forget her children. To use the word *Abba* is to use that tenderest of terms to describe Father God, "papa,"[1] one used by those who know Him intimately.

Some of us may not have had healthy relationships with our parents, so the idea of God as a parent may not bring immediate comfort and joy. Yet, any and all good impulses we have toward our children or those who are weaker than us are from God. When we incline, when we bend toward those who are needy, we are imitating our Father God. He sees the needy; He has the heart of an adoptive father because He is one. Psalm 68:5 describes God as the "Father of the fatherless."

> Think for a moment: why might God have used parental imagery to tell us about Himself and how we are to relate to Him?

> What emotions or imagery do these parental analogies bring to your mind? Explain.

"Father" is one of the many names God calls Himself. Let's quickly look at the first time in Scripture God was renamed by a person and the first time He revealed His name to man.

> READ Genesis 16:1-13. What are the circumstances of God's messenger finding Hagar? Why is the messenger's appearing and pronouncement of blessing so surprising?

Note: When you read "angel of the LORD" in verse 7, the Hebrew word for "angel" here is *malak*, which means "a messenger."[2] This could be a human messenger or an angelic one, but either way, this messenger has been sent by God.

Scholars aren't sure whether this messenger was God Himself or simply an angel who had been sent by God with the authority to speak God's words as his own. I find it interesting how God often sends a messenger, or shows up as a man, and then that messenger or man turns out to be God in disguise, for lack of a better word. (See Gen. 18 and Gen. 32:22-32 for other examples.) The whole thing is such a mystery, and I've learned that, as believers, we must learn to be OK with mystery.

Below, record what Hagar says to God and about God in verse 13.

Hagar, an Egyptian slave woman, was the first and only person in the Bible to rename God. Think about that for a moment. She was the first and only person to give God a name, and the name she chose was, "You are a God of seeing" (Gen. 16:13). And the reason she gave? "Truly here I have seen him who looks after me." She was also the first person who "the angel of the LORD" visited and one of the first people whose cry God heard and answered, as recorded in the Bible.

What does Hagar's story in Genesis 16 tell you about God?

If God saw the plight of an Egyptian slave those many years ago, surely He sees you and He sees me in our difficulties.

**READ** Exodus 3:1-14, and explain God's main message to Moses.

What name did God reveal to Moses in verse 14?

Moses asked God what Moses should say if the Israelites questioned him as to who sent Moses to rescue them from slavery. God replied in verse 14 that He is "I AM WHO I AM," 'ehyeh or hayah hayah, meaning, "I am the one who is and who will be present with you and for you."[3] He is the One who is and who will be. Then God commanded Moses to tell the people that He is "the LORD," Yahweh (YHWH, Adonai), the personal name of God, meaning "He will be."[4]

God is saying that He is and He always has been. Hebrew scholar Chaim Bentorah says,

> The word YHWH expressing the name of God in Hebrew is built on three words; hayah which means "was," hoveh which means "is" and yiheyeh which means "will be." This is to say that God lives in the past, present and future simultaneously.[5]

What does knowing the meaning of God's name help us to understand about how He interacts with our lives?

Does God's eternal presence bring you comfort? Why or why not?

Let's turn now to the New Testament to see a mention of God's messenger, "the angel of the LORD," visiting someone after God heard the man's prayers.

**READ** Luke 1:5-17,24-25. What can we know about Zechariah and Elizabeth from this passage?

Consider the stories we've studied today. How does God's mercy and clear care for His children encourage you in the circumstances or places of your heart that seem hidden? Write a quick prayer of praise to God for His loving care for us, His children.

God so often makes Himself known to us in our afflictions.

When we get hurt or are sad, God inclines to us—a parent to His children. We don't always see it at first, but He's there bringing light and working for our good, comforting in ways that time usually reveals as we look back. Are we eagerly watching for Him?

Answers often come in time—healing work done over years. Sometimes we can only see it in the rearview mirrors of our lives. Then we know. He was faithful. He was gentle. He inclined to me and heard my cry. Those moments of grace, when we see His working in the past remind us that He will be for us in the future. He will be faithful. He will be gentle. I AM, who has always been and will always be, bookends our existence with His goodness and love.

The tender mercy of the thing is, He didn't just bend down—He came down.

We'll talk about this more in our next session.

How did God speak to you today?

What's your response to Him?

## 2

# *HE COMES TO US*

⁶ In sacrifice and offering you have not delighted, but you have given me an open ear. Burnt offering and sin offering you have not required. ⁷ Then I said, "Behold, I have come; in the scroll of the book it is written of me: ⁸ I delight to do your will, O my God; your law is within my heart."

**PSALM 40:6-8**

Before we begin, pray a prayer like this:

*Father God, open my mind so that I may understand the Scriptures, and my eyes that I may behold wondrous things in Your Word.*

This is going to be a wild session. We're going to study Hebrews 10:1-18 today. But, first, let's talk a bit about the Old Testament sacrificial system.

On a scale of 1-10, with 1 being *Barely Heard of Them* and 10 being *Very Knowledgeable About Them*, how would you rate your understanding of the Old Testament sacrificial system and law?
1      2      3      4      5      6      7      8      9      10
*Barely Heard of Them*                    *Very Knowledgeable About Them*

## SACRIFICES AND OFFERINGS

Because we don't practice the Old Testament sacrificial system today, it can be easy to write it off as irrelevant to us. Yet, there are some beautiful truths tucked into the purpose and meaning behind the sacrificial system that God can use to teach us today.

> **READ** Leviticus 1:3-4 and 17:11. Record below what God says the burnt offering will do for His people.

The word *atonement* (*kaphar*) means to cover or make reconciliation.

> **READ** Hebrews 9:22. Based on this passage, is there any forgiveness of sin without the shedding of blood?

In very simplified terms, the Old Testament sacrificial system was meant to help God's people understand a few key ideas (among others): God is holy. Man is sinful. God cannot be associated with sin. But, God loves His children. So He created a way for His people to get rid of their sins (atone for them), so they could be in fellowship with Him. God provided very specific guidelines for sacrifices to help His people atone for sin, so they could worship Him in His temple—a place that was meant to represent God's dwelling place among His children.

God also gave His children the law. Let's be honest, the Old Testament law can seem weirdly specific and strange to our twenty-first century ears. Suffice it to say, in His law, God was showing us some of His nature and explaining to His people how He created them to live in their day and context. Because God made the world and every man and woman, He also understands how He made us to live. By giving us His law, He was telling us how to flourish. However, because we are fallen men and women, we can never obey all of God's law perfectly. Through God's law, we come to understand our sinfulness and our need for Him.

The sacrificial system was put in place for times when God's people had broken His law. Because they could never perfectly follow God's law, God's people were continually giving burnt offerings and sacrifices to make reconciliation. Yet, these burnt offerings and sacrifices could never ultimately make people right with God. They were only temporary fixes. The sacrificial system and the law pointed to a final reconciliation with God, through Christ.

**READ** Hebrews 10:1-18.

Focus on Hebrews 10:1,4. If the law can't "make perfect those who draw near" and "it is impossible for the blood of bulls and goats to take away sins," what does Hebrews 10 offer instead as the solution for that sin?

Look at verses 11-14. In contrast to the sacrificial system, how often does the sacrifice of Jesus need to be performed?

Now, look at verses 15-17. How does the Holy Spirit play a part in our process of being sanctified?

What does Jesus' sacrifice on our behalf mean for us as followers of Christ?

The law and sacrifices of the Old Testament point to the need for a Savior. That need was met once and for all in Jesus' perfect sacrifice for us on the cross. Jesus bore the full weight of our sins and satisfied God's holy judgment forever. If we have submitted our lives to God, He sees Jesus' righteousness as our own. And, more than that, He has given us the Holy Spirit, who has taken up residence in our hearts. The Holy Spirit not only bears witness that we are God's children (Rom. 8:16), but He enables us to live in a way that is pleasing to God.

He puts God's laws on our hearts and writes them on our minds (Heb. 10:16). Before salvation, we were controlled by our flesh without a way to say no to sin. But, because of Jesus' sacrifice for us, we can now choose to walk in the Spirit, choose to walk in a way that is pleasing to God—in the light. We can choose to agree with God about how He made us and walk in the paths that lead to flourishing.

God inclined to His people in the Old Testament times, giving them the sacrificial system and law, and by dwelling among them in the temple. God inclined to His people in the New Testament times by sending His Son, Jesus, to live among us and provide a sacrifice to make us right with Him. God inclines to us today through the sacrifice of Jesus and the Holy Spirit who indwells our hearts when we receive Christ as Lord. (See also Jer. 31:31-33.)

Reread Hebrews 10:18, and paraphrase the verse in your own words.

How does understanding this verse bring you hope?

We'll continue our discussion of Hebrews 10 tomorrow. There's a beautiful correlation that you won't want to miss.

## ③

# HE COMES TO US, PART 2

> <sup>6</sup> In sacrifice and offering you have not delighted, but you have given me an open ear. Burnt offering and sin offering you have not required. <sup>7</sup> Then I said, "Behold, I have come; in the scroll of the book it is written of me: <sup>8</sup> I delight to do your will, O my God; your law is within my heart."
>
> ### PSALM 40:6-8

Before we begin, pray a prayer like this:

*Father God, open my mind so that I may understand the Scriptures, and my eyes that I may behold wondrous things in Your Word.*

Yesterday, as you were reading Hebrews 10:1-18, did any of the verses sound familiar to you? You may have noticed a marked similarity between Psalm 40:6-8 and Hebrews 10:5-7. The New Testament writer of Hebrews applied this Old Testament text from Psalm 40 to speak of Jesus' coming.

Remember from our discussion of God's choosing and anointing of David as king that God called David "a man after his own heart" (1 Sam. 13:14)? In 2 Samuel 7:16, God told David, through Nathan the prophet: "Your house and your kingdom shall be made sure forever before me. Your throne shall be established forever." This prophecy is ultimately fulfilled in the coming of Jesus, who was born in the earthly line of David and who is and will be our eternal king (Luke 1:32).

Look at Psalm 40:6-8 and Hebrews 10:5-7 below.

<sup>6</sup> In sacrifice and offering you have not delighted,
but you have given me an open ear.
Burnt offering and sin offering
you have not required.
<sup>7</sup> Then I said, "Behold, I have come;
in the scroll of the book it is written of me:
<sup>8</sup> I delight to do your will, O my God;
your law is within my heart."

**PSALM 40:6-8**

<sup>5</sup> Consequently, when Christ came into the world, he said,
"Sacrifices and offerings you have not desired,
but a body have you prepared for me;
<sup>6</sup> in burnt offerings and sin offerings
you have taken no pleasure.
<sup>7</sup> Then I said, 'Behold, I have come to do your will, O God,
as it is written of me in the scroll of the book.'"

**HEBREWS 10:5-7**

Take a few moments to study them.
□ Highlight the sentences that are the same.
□ Underline the sentences, words, and phrases that are different.

Let's study the differences in these passages that carry the mystery of the human and the divine.

## *AN OPEN EAR*

In Psalm 40:6, David wrote, "you have given me an open ear."

> We've been considering these verses for a few days now. Write below what you think the phrase "you have given me an open ear" might mean.

The literal rendering of this phrase in Hebrew is "my ear you have dug" or "you pierced my ear." What could this mean practically? Scholar Gerald Wilson explains, "this [phrase] would yield the sense of 'open up' ears or 'dig (new) ears' so that one can hear. The new openness acquired by the psalmist through God's action is apparently mirrored in his willingness to do the divine will (40:8)."[6] This phrase is "a symbol of being attentive to Yahweh in order to obey Him ... [emphasizing] the importance of obedience."[7] So, here, it seems that David was praising God for giving him an ear to understand God's ways and a willingness to walk in obedience.

> List some ways God has opened your ears in the past, maybe through specific passages of Scripture, friends, or circumstances.

> Have there been times in your life when you didn't want to have an open ear before God? Are you in one of those times now? Explain.

## A BODY PREPARED

You noticed, I'm sure, that the words in Hebrews 10:5 "a body you have pre-pared for me" are a bit different from the second line of Psalm 40:6, "you have given me an open ear." What accounts for this difference? Many scholars believe it has to do with a difference in translation and language of the source used in the original transcripts of the text. Yet, scholars say that this variance in language still communicates a similar core message.[8] David L. Allen says, "Only by means of the incarnation can Jesus accomplish the will of God to do away with sin. ... The open ear and the yielded body both signify obedience to the will of God."[9]

## DELIGHTING TO DO GOD'S WILL

Psalm 40:8 says, "I delight to do your will" while Hebrews 10:7 reads, "I have come to do your will." I don't think it's an accident that the passage has changed. One commentator says the author of Hebrews probably made these changes to his quotation of the Psalm 40 passage for emphasis and to show the relation of the text to Jesus.[10]

It's interesting that in the Hebrews passage, the language construction used for "'I have come.' 'To do your will, O God' is emphatic."[11] So, it's not that David delighted to do God's will and Jesus doesn't. In fact, Jesus delights to do God's will more than David ever could have; Jesus was and is one with God the Father. I love the way one scholar says it: "'I have come to do your will' is written over the whole record of our Lord's life; this was his attitude from first to last."[12] The more emphatic and focused construction of "I have come to do your will" points to the fact that Jesus came to earth with the expressed purpose of doing God's will.

> In your own words, how would you characterize the difference between Jesus' "I have come to do your will" and David's "I delight to do your will"?

> Do you usually delight to do God's will? If not, what keeps you from it? Explain.

# THE SCROLL OF THE BOOK

There is no clear consensus on the exact meaning of the phrase "in the scroll of the book it is written of me" in Psalm 40:7. Some believe it refers to Deuteronomy 17:14-20, the laws God gave Israel's kings, to honor Him above all else.[13] Some believe that it refers to a heavenly book where the deeds of people were recorded.[14] And some believe it's a more general reference to the Old Testament law that the psalmist observed. Scholar Gerald Wilson says, "whatever solution one chooses, it seems clear that the psalmist, having experienced a new awareness and understanding as a result of the divine opening of his ears, now perceives the 'scroll' as speaking directly to his circumstance. As a result he becomes willing to do Yahweh's will."[15]

I'm grateful for the rhythm of grace that God shows us here. If we follow this psalm, here's where it takes us. 1) God opens our ears and gives us understanding of His will. 2) God helps us to understand that He delights in contrite and obedient hearts more than sacrifices or showy external displays of piety. 3) He gives us His instruction in His Word. He helps us see how His Word applies to our lives and everyday circumstances. He enables us to desire to obey Him and helps us to actually obey Him by the power of His Spirit.

> Take a moment to consider the rhythm of grace we've identified above. Is there a particular part of this pattern that comes more difficultly to you? Explain.

> Ask God to help you surrender that area to Him.

David and Jesus were both willing servants of the Lord—David, through his life commitment, and Jesus, all the way through His death and resurrection. But Jesus not only served His Father through the submission of His will and the surrender of His equality with God—He chose to empty Himself and wear flesh to serve us (Phil. 2:5-10). God as a servant! For us, God came down to earth incarnate (embodied in flesh) and made a way for our cries to one day no longer exist.

This Hebrews quotation of Psalm 40 shows us that the sacrifice of Jesus' body was infinitely superior to any of the offerings the law had previously defined. It shows us how Jesus' once-and-for-all sacrifice has secured our eternal relationship with God and ultimately the forgiveness of our sins.

## *OUR HUMAN RESPONSE*

David found delight in God's will, and he kept God's instruction within his heart so he could obey Him. He knew that to God obedience was better than sacrifice (Ps. 51:16-17). We see this same sentiment echoed in Hebrews 10.

God's desire for us toward Him is the same as what He offers us: steadfast love that reveals itself through action. Love. Obedience. Steadfast. Never-ending, keeping-on in praise and through pain.

> Spend a few moments in a time of prayer—responding to God in light of our study today. Feel free to journal your prayer below.

# 4

# *OUR GENTLE FATHER*

### Behold, I have come …
#### PSALM 40:7

Before we begin, pray a prayer like this:

*Father God, open my mind so that I may understand the Scriptures, and my eyes that I may behold wondrous things in Your Word.*

I love those words, "I have come." I think of a teenager, maybe at a party, who gets into some trouble. She calls her dad, who she knows will help her, even in her mess. Her dad shows up at the party without a minute to spare and says, "I'm here." It's going to be OK, because her dad is there to rescue her.

This is how I view God, our Father. He comes to us in the mess we—and others—have made of our lives and the lives around us, and He says, "I'm here." He tells us to get in the car, so to speak, so He can drive us home safely.

> But to all who did receive him, who believed in his name,
> he gave the right to become children of God.

#### JOHN 1:12

In this session, I want to talk about God, our rescuer, as our gentle Father. First, I'd like to note three stand-out things I've learned about God in my studies in the Old and New Testaments:

1. **GOD HATES REBELLION, WHICH STEMS FROM PRIDE (THINKING WE KNOW BETTER THAN HE DOES).** He is jealous for the love of His people and hates when they turn to anything or anyone other than Him. Think of the first and greatest commandment: "You shall love the LORD your God with all your heart and with all your soul and with all your mind" (Matt. 22:37-38).

2. **GOD IS SO TENDER AND COMPASSIONATE TOWARD HIS PEOPLE, MAKING A WAY FOR US TO COME BACK TO HIM OVER AND OVER AGAIN.** He makes a way for us to trust Him in humility, to remember who He is. Humility, truly understanding our need for God and our state without Him, helps us get to God. When we come to Him in our need, He will help us with His fullness.

3. **GOD IS ALWAYS FOR THE POOR, THE NEEDY, THE AFFLICTED, THE MISTREATED, AND THE OPPRESSED.** We see Him again and again in Scripture protecting those who are hurting or cast aside.

The Old and New Testaments strongly reveal each of these qualities of God.

God is so tender and compassionate toward us. I am particularly struck by His gentleness with us—He is so powerful, He could easily crush us, but He's not rough with us. In fact, the opposite is true.

> When you think of the word *gentle*, what comes to mind? Positive or negative emotions? Is there a certain person you think of? A certain image or circumstance? Explain.

> **READ** Psalm 18:35.

The word for "gentleness" here in Hebrew is *anavah*, which calls to mind *humility or meekness.*

> Why do you think David would say that the Lord's gentleness made him great?

**READ** Romans 2:4. God's kindness, His gentleness, leads us to repentance. How have you seen this in your own life?

**READ** Matthew 11:30.

God's kindness leads us to repentance. And that same kindness shapes the way that He leads us day by day, the way that He offers us guidance in life and rest in walking with Him.

## *THE GENTLENESS OF GOD*

God is mighty. He is strong. He is portrayed like a lion able to tear apart and terrify. He is our strength, our Rock, and our Fortress. He is not weak. He is the ultimate victor. Even though He has all power and strength and might, He is also gentle and humble and kind; He is both strong and meek, all-powerful and humble, a lion and a lamb.

**READ** Isaiah 40:1-11.

To lend a bit of context to your study of this passage, Isaiah, after the excruciating judgment God's people had endured in exile, was now bringing good news to "Jerusalem" (the people of God), who were in Babylonian captivity.

We don't have space here to detail exactly how and why God's people were taken into captivity. For our purposes, just know that God warned His people for many years to repent of their sins and the ways that they were walking contrary to Him. He sent prophets to lead them back to Himself, and they wouldn't listen. He told them that they would be judged if they didn't repent. God allowed foreign powers to conquer His people and take them into exile as judgment, just as He said He would. After years of being displaced and treated as slaves in a foreign land, now, finally, a prophecy of hope. God told His people what was wouldn't always be; the Lord was rescuing His people.

What did God plan to do for His people, and how did He tell Isaiah to speak to Jerusalem (vv. 1-2)?

Notice the word "recompense" in verse 10. Look up the definition and write it below.

What do you think it might look like for Jesus to have "his recompense before him" (v. 10)?

Who do you think Jesus was describing when He said He would gather the lambs in His arms? (Hint: see Ps. 100:3.)

How will He lead those who are with young (literally, those who are nursing)?

READ the following passages of Scripture. Beside each, record what the text tells you about Jesus' nature or His actions.

Matthew 11:29

John 10:11

2 Corinthians 10:1

Philippians 2:8

When we encounter the gentle nature of Jesus, we're encountering the caring character of God.

Have you ever really thought of gentleness as one of God's traits? Explain.

The tender love of God is seen throughout Scripture.

Do you think of gentleness as an admirable quality? Do you strive to be gentle with others and yourself? Why or why not?

One last thing to note before we close out this session. Notice the word *behold* in both Psalm 40:7 and Isaiah 40:9. This Hebrew word used here is trying to get your attention.[16] It's saying, "Stop and look. Pay attention!"

"Behold, your God!"
"Behold, I have come"

Pay attention to your God, to the One who comes to the party where you're ashamed, let down, deceived, and, no questions asked, says, "I'm here. I have come to make sure you're OK."

This is your Father. He comes to you. He inclines down to care for you. Do you see?

Look up to where He inclined to us on the cross-shaped altar of sacrifice. The gentle, meek, humble God-man who didn't roar like a lion, but bled as a lamb, the final offering for our sins. And then, the defeat of death: Resurrection! New life after death.

What's your response to God today?

SESSION FIVE:

# LIFTED AND STEADIED

He drew me up from the pit of destruction,
out of the miry bog,
and set my feet upon a rock,
making my steps secure.

**PSALM 40:2**

# GROUP GUIDE

**WARM THINGS UP**

Here are a few questions to begin your time.

> Think of the Bible passages we read on Day 1 of last session (the stories of Hagar, Moses, and Elizabeth and Zechariah). Which of these stories resonated with you most? Explain.

> Is it hard for you to believe that God sees you? Why or why not?

> Share a time when God inclined down to you and heard your cry. Explain the circumstances and how you saw Him act on your behalf.

> Jesus was the final sacrifice who ended the need for a sacrificial system and makes you right with God forever. How does this truth affect the way you relate to God and others on a daily basis?

> What do you think of gentleness? Is it easy for you to see God's gentleness to you? Explain.

**WATCH**

To view Session Five's teaching from Sarah Mae, download the optional video bundle at LifeWay.com/Psalm40.

**CREATE CONVERSATION**

> Do you have trouble asking others for help? Explain.

> Do you have trouble asking God for help? Explain.

> Suffering (the pit) can be a place of pain and a place of providence. Can you remember a hard situation that led you to God? Explain.

Close your time with prayer, asking God to remind us of His faithfulness to lift us out of situations and help us overcome sin struggles that we can't fix on our own. Make sure to ask if anyone has a specific prayer need this week.

# 1

# *THE METAPHOR OF THE MUDDY PIT*

## He drew me up from the pit of destruction, out of the miry bog ...

### PSALM 40:2

Before we begin, pray a prayer like this:

*Father God, open my mind so that I may understand the Scriptures, and my eyes that I may behold wondrous things in Your Word.*

Much of Hebrew poetry employs the use of metaphor. In this session we're going to explore the illustrative language and imagery David used to express what his life was like. We're going to employ some of these same tools in our own lives to describe the painful and sometimes horrid experiences we've had.

First, let's define some terms.

Look up these words in a dictionary, and write the definitions below:

Pit

Miry

Bog

The word for "pit" here in Psalm 40:2 means *cistern*. A cistern "is a large hole dug in the ground (usually in bedrock) that is designed to store rainwater. It differs from a well significantly in that it only holds captured rainwater, as opposed to tapping into an underground water source, as do wells."[1]

After 1300 BC, plaster was put into cisterns in order to make sure rain water didn't seep into the ground. Cisterns ranged from very large to being narrow and deep. Picture a hole in the ground, about twenty inches wide (if that), and up to seventy-five feet in length.[2] If you were to stand over it and look down, you'd see that the deeper it goes, the darker it gets.[3]

> Now that you have the proper image of a cistern in your mind, read the Scriptures below.
>
> Genesis 37:20-24
>
> Jeremiah 38:1-6
>
> What happened to both of these men?
>
> Why did Joseph's brothers throw him in a pit (Gen. 37:3-8)?
>
> Why did the officials throw Jeremiah in a pit (Jer. 38:4)?

This wasn't the first time Jeremiah had been imprisoned. (See Jer. 37:11-20 if you want to read about it.) We'll revisit Joseph's and Jeremiah's stories next session, so keep them in mind.

## PIT OF DESTRUCTION

To understand the phrase "pit of destruction," we need to take a look at the Hebrew, because the word "destruction" conveys something very specific. The Hebrew word used here is *sha'own*, and it means an "uproar (as of rushing); by implication, destruction" or the "roar (of water)."[4]

**READ** the passages below, noticing where the word *sha'own* is used.

Who stills the roaring (*sha'own*) of the seas,
the roaring (*sha'own*) of their waves,
the tumult of the peoples ...

**PSALM 65:7**

Ah, the thunder of many peoples; they thunder like the thundering of the sea! Ah, the roar (*sha'own*) of nations; they roar like the roaring (*sha'own*) of mighty waters!

**ISAIAH 17:12**

This roaring and rushing is horrible and tumultuous.

Close your eyes and picture a pit, a long, narrow, dark cistern, where the bottom is muddy and swampy. Now put yourself in that pit. Imagine trying to move around as your feet get stuck in the mire. Suddenly rushing water thrashes over you, a storm has descended. You try and grasp the walls of the pit, but the plaster has softened in the rain and it slides between your fingertips—there is nothing to grasp. You're not only stuck, but you keep getting knocked over by the rush of water. You can't steady yourself, and you can barely catch your breath. You're terrified. But there's no way you're getting out of this pit unless someone comes along and pulls you out.

With this image in mind, write down a few words that communicate how David likely felt to have written such a graphic metaphor. I'll give you one to get started.

David likely felt:
*Stuck*

# *EXPRESSION AND INSIGHT THROUGH METAPHOR*

I'm going to ask you to do something that might hurt.

Before I do, I want to tell you what I mean by the word *insight*. I'm talking about discovering something, a truth, that you didn't see before. This kind of insight is a revealing or uncovering, and sometimes it comes when we're willing to think and process in a way that we haven't done before.

> With this in mind, I want you to think of one of the hardest times in your life. In the space below, write a metaphor for what that time for you was like. What did it feel like? What did you see? How did it smell? What did you hear? What did it taste like? Remember, a metaphor is naming something tangible to explain the intangible. I acknowledge that this might be painful to relive. My hope is expressing yourself through metaphor may offer some insight and relief.

God helps those who can't help themselves, who can't pull themselves up and out of a pit by their bootstraps. We're all dependent on God's mercy every day.

> How did God speak to you today?

> What's your response to Him?

**2**

# THE PIT OF PAIN AND PROVIDENCE

## He drew me up from the pit of destruction, out of the miry bog ...

### PSALM 40:2

Before we begin, pray a prayer like this:

*Father God, open my mind so that I may understand the Scriptures, and my eyes that I may behold wondrous things in Your Word.*

Look up the word *providence*, and write the definition below.

The Greek meaning of *providence* is "forethought, provident care ... to make provision," considering in advance.[5] When we talk about God's providence in our lives, we're talking about how He has given thought to us (Ps. 40:5,17), He has seen our stories before they even began (Ps. 139:16; Jer. 1:5; Eph. 2:10), and He acts and makes provision for us based on what He knows, to make us look more like Himself and to free us for Himself (Matt. 6:31-32; Rom. 8:28; Phil. 4:19).

Let's revisit the stories of Joseph and Jeremiah.

> **READ** Genesis 37:25-28. What did Joseph's brothers happen to see as they sat down to eat? Who interceded on Joseph's behalf?

Part of the reason Joseph's brothers hated him, apart from Joseph's poorly timed idea to share his dreams, was that Jacob, Joseph's father, favored Joseph above his brothers. And Jacob wasn't shy about showing that favoritism—giving Joseph preferential treatment and even that famous coat of many colors. If you're familiar with the story of Rachel and Leah, Joseph was Jacob's favorite largely because he was Rachel's son. Rachel was Jacob's favored wife, the one who had his heart.

After Joseph was sold into slavery, he didn't see his family again for at least twenty years. Joseph was seventeen when his brothers sold him (Gen. 37:2). You're likely familiar with Joseph's story, but let's quickly review some of the big moments of his life. Unfortunately, being sold into slavery wasn't the worst thing to happen to Joseph. There was more to come.

**POTIPHAR'S HOUSE:** In Genesis 39, we're told that Joseph was sold as a slave in Egypt to work in the house of Potiphar, an officer of the Pharaoh. God was with Joseph and prospered the work of his hands, so much so that Potiphar made Joseph the overseer of his house, putting him in charge of everything that Potiphar owned. Things seemed to be going well, until Potiphar's wife was attracted to Joseph and attempted to seduce him. The biblical account implies that her advances were continuous, over time, and at every turn, Joseph resisted. One day, however, she grabbed Joseph by a piece of his clothing to try to persuade him to sleep with her. He fled the house, with her still holding his clothing in hand. She then accused Joseph of coming on to her. Potiphar had Joseph thrown in jail, the prison where the king's prisoners were confined, an act of leniency, as typically a slave would have been killed for such a crime.

**PRISON:** Though imprisoned for a crime he didn't commit, Joseph continued to prosper under the Lord's hand. The overseer of the prison put Joseph in charge of every prisoner there. One day, Pharaoh sent his chief cupbearer and chief baker to prison. While there, both prisoners had dreams and Joseph, through God's enabling, interpreted those dreams. Joseph's dream interpretation came true. The chief baker was killed, but the chief cupbearer was restored to Pharaoh's court. Joseph asked the chief cupbearer to remember Joseph when the cupbearer was back in Pharaoh's good graces, in the hopes that Pharaoh could release Joseph from jail. The chief cupbearer did not remember Joseph. And for two whole years Joseph continued working in the prison, seemingly unseen. Then, Pharaoh needed a dream interpreted, and his cupbearer remembered Joseph.

**PHARAOH'S SERVICE:** Pharaoh called Joseph from the prison to explain a dream Pharaoh had. God gave Joseph the dream's interpretation: there would be seven years of plenty in Egypt, followed by seven years of famine. Joseph advised Pharaoh to choose a man to oversee the seven years of plenty, to store the extra harvest so that the Egyptians would have plenty in the seven years of famine. Pharaoh agreed with what God had said, and he appointed Joseph to be that overseer. Joseph wisely managed the years of plenty, and during the years of famine, people from all over the region came to him for food. Some of those people were Joseph's brothers and father.

    **READ** Genesis 45:6-7, and write verse 7 below.

There was purpose in Joseph's pain, a providential purpose, that God wove together for the good of His people over those twenty years. Evil made a play, but God always writes the ultimate story, and it's a story for our good and God's glory.

We'll talk about evil more soon. But first, let's look at a heart-wrenching and beautiful moment in this redemption story.

After everything, finally, finally, Joseph got to see his beloved father again, and Israel (Jacob) got to see his beloved son again, the one he had wept for and lamented over—believing Joseph to be dead. They saw each other and (picture this), Joseph threw his arms around his father's neck, falling into him, and wept for a long time (Gen. 46:29).

Sit with that moment. Consider it in your mind's eye—a beloved son reunited with his father after years of heartache and struggle.

After years of difficulty and missing his father desperately, what was Joseph's conclusion about it all? (See Gen. 50:19-20.)

Despite enduring trial after trial, Joseph remained faithful to God. You can read more of Joseph's story in Genesis 37–50.

## JEREMIAH'S STORY

Jeremiah was alive in a particularly difficult time in Israel's history. As we briefly discussed last session, God had told the Israelites living in Judah that they were going to be taken into captivity by Babylon. It was a judgment for the ways the people had continued to rebel against God, despite His loving calls to repent. Jeremiah lived in Jerusalem while the Babylonians sieged the city. They would eventually capture the city and take some of its people into exile in Babylon. This was the last bit of the conflict before the exile.[6]

God had told Jeremiah to advise King Zedekiah to surrender to the Babylonians. Many of the government officials were already angry at Jeremiah, saying that he was being cowardly and his words were discouraging the soldiers who were to fight against the Babylonians. They were so angry, in fact, that they had Jeremiah placed in that cistern.[7]

**READ** Jeremiah 38:7-13. Who interceded for Jeremiah?

**READ** Jeremiah 38:14-28. After Jeremiah was rescued, what did he do?

Jeremiah continued with the call the Lord had given him. He didn't quit. He kept on in obedience.

Do you find it hard to continue in obedience when things get difficult? Explain.

Respond to each prompt below including examples from your own life.

A time when God turned evil for your good:

An evil you're now asking God to redeem:

## THE BATTLE IS REAL

There's an entire spiritual realm alive and active around us that God has not allowed us to see. Believers do not have to fear. We're told that if we resist the devil, "he will flee" from us (Jas. 4:7). God helps us by the power of His Holy Spirit. However, we have reason to be on guard (1 Pet. 5:8) and prepared (Eph. 6:10-20).

## HE WILL DELIVER

Because life in this world doesn't unfold how we'd always like it to unfold, it's tempting to doubt the promises of God. I know I do this, especially when it comes to deliverance. Will God really deliver in a tangible way? Can I tell people He really will deliver?

Joseph was delivered from his time as a slave and a prisoner; however, as we read, it was years before he rose to power in Pharaoh's household. And it was twenty years before Joseph reconciled with his father and brothers.

The line of Adam was offered deliverance from sin, through Jesus, but it took thousands of years before that deliverance came.

Deliverance is real. Sometimes it comes to fruition on this earth the way it came for Joseph—in physical deliverance and comfort. But it always comes for our souls. God is always redeeming and delivering our souls. Yes, if we're followers of Christ, our souls will be redeemed eternally. But even here on earth God is sanctifying us, making our souls reflect more of His character. Through soul change, there is life change—even if some of our prayers are not answered the way we hope.

And yet, we still and always pray and hope.

## *OUR LIFE IS IN HIS LOVING HANDS*

I'll never forget a prayer that a mentor of mine taught me to pray in regard to my children and the fears that a mother carries for her children: *Lord, I pray that nothing would happen to my children that hasn't first gone through your loving hands.*

I've clung to that prayer of trust over the years, as my children have gone through painful times. After a terrible thing happened to one of my children, another mentor-friend told me, "This is a part of your child's story. God can work good out of it in your child's life."

No matter what happens to us or the people we love, God is always working for the good of those who love Him, no matter the circumstance, no matter the story.

> As for you, O LORD, you will not restrain your mercy from me;
> your steadfast love and your faithfulness will ever preserve me!

### PSALM 40:11

Remember, God uses all things for our good, even evil. In His providence, He makes provision concerning us and His people as a whole. We matter to Him individually and as a body of believers. The key is to remember that what we don't know, He knows. What we don't see, He sees. And where we feel lost and confused, He is certain.

**3**

# *ONTO THE ROCK*

He drew me up from the pit of destruction,
out of the miry bog,
and set my feet upon a rock,
making my steps secure.

**PSALM 40:2**

Before we begin, pray a prayer like this:

*Father God, open my mind so that I may understand the Scriptures, and my eyes that I may behold wondrous things in Your Word.*

God is called a Rock many times throughout the Scriptures. Beside each passage below, write how God is described as our Rock in the text.

Deuteronomy 32:4

Deuteronomy 32:17-19

2 Samuel 22:2

Psalm 28:1

The words for *rock* in these Scriptures signify a large rock, cliff, or crag.

Look up the word *crag* in the dictionary, and write the definition below. Look up a picture of one as well.

Why would you use a rock as a metaphor for God? What do you think? What is it about a rock, or crag, that would cause someone to say God is like one?

## THE CORNERSTONE

**READ** Ephesians 2:11-22. What's a cornerstone? Look it up.

For those of us who aren't contractors, *cornerstone* may be a bit of an unfamiliar term. A *cornerstone* is, a "stone laid at the corner to bind two walls together and to strengthen them."[8]

Looking back at Ephesians 2, how is Jesus the cornerstone?

**READ** Isaiah 28:16. What kind of stone is laid in Zion? Who laid it?

For years, God prophesied that He would provide a cornerstone for His people. In Zechariah 10:3-4, God said that He would provide a cornerstone for His people from the tribe of Judah. As we discussed earlier, Jesus is from the line of David, which just happens to be, you guessed it, in the tribe of Judah. (See Matt. 1:1-6.)

Write the last line of Isaiah 28:16.

The last line of verse 16, "Whoever believes will not be in haste," seems a bit cryptic at first glance. Scholars say here in "the meaning of the Hebrew, haste and hurry [are] being regarded in their contrast to the calm temper of a steadfast faith."[9] Another scholar says, "the Greek OT interprets this Hebrew verb for hurry in the sense of 'put to shame.'"[10] In other words, whoever believes in this cornerstone will not be put to shame, but have the peace of a steadfast faith, anchored in Christ's final sacrifice.

READ Psalm 118:22-23, and write it below in your own words.

Jesus was the prophesied cornerstone who would come to make reconciliation between God and all people. He came to His people and they rejected Him. While on earth, Jesus was discredited and despised by the scribes and Pharisees, the most religious people, because they thought the Messiah would not look or act like Jesus looked or acted when He came. They expected a powerful political and religious figure, not the humble Savior who came and died on a cross to save us all.

Let's revisit Ephesians 2:11-22. What does it say about the Gentiles, those of us who are not part of Israel, the Jewish people?

This mystery is that the Gentiles are fellow heirs,
members of the same body, and partakers of the
promise in Christ Jesus through the gospel.

**EPHESIANS 3:6**

$^{28}$ As regards the gospel, they are enemies for your sake. But as regards to election, they are beloved for the sake of their forefathers. $^{29}$ For the gifts and the calling of God are irrevocable. $^{30}$ For just as you were at one time disobedient to God but now have received mercy because of their disobedience, $^{31}$ so they too have now been disobedient in order that by the mercy shown to you they also may now receive mercy. $^{32}$ For God has consigned all to disobedience, that he may have mercy on all.

**ROMANS 11:28-32**

It's crucial to note here that God's people, Israel, also known as the Jews, are in covenant with God. He loves them. And it's only by His mercy that we, Gentiles, are grafted in to be His people, His children. There is a mystery here we don't understand when it comes to Israel. What we do know is that all throughout history, God has come for His people, rescuing them and redeeming them. As newly grafted in branches, we are to love our Jewish neighbors well and to pray earnestly for them to know Jesus as Messiah.

If you're a Gentile, think about God's kindness in grafting you into the body of Christ. Write a short prayer of praise below.

## *OUR FIRM FOUNDATION*

God the Father is our Rock. Jesus is the Cornerstone, the foundation that holds us all together and steadies us. The Holy Spirit leads and guides us into all truth. They all anchor us and hold us securely, both now and eternally. We need all three.

Never forget the firm foundation you have in God. Times will come—or perhaps they already have—that will cause you to feel as though you're sinking. When the deep waters come, and everyone is telling you to swim harder, God knows you need someone to come alongside you, throw out a lifeline, and pull you safely back to dry land. In these times of trouble, our metaphorical dry land can look differently.

Dry land can come in the form of actual help from people, letting others help you when the waters are too deep for you to navigate on your own. God often uses others to comfort His children. Dry land can come in the form of the foundation that we have in Christ. A truth that we often need to be reminded of.

We need to know the words of Isaiah 43:1-3 that tells us:

> ¹ But now thus says the LORD,
> he who created you, O Jacob,
> he who formed you, O Israel:
> "Fear not, for I have redeemed you;
> I have called you by name, you are mine.
> ² When you pass through the waters, *I will be with you;*
> and through the rivers, they shall not *overwhelm you;*
> (it will not take you away in its flood; it will not
> drown you) when you walk through fire *you*
> *shall not be burned,* (burned up)
> and *the flame shall not consume you.*
> ³ For I am the LORD your God,
> the Holy One of Israel, *your Savior ...*"

### ISAIAH 43:1-3 (italics and parenthetical notes mine)

Which of the promises from Isaiah 43 above is most precious to you?

Isaiah 43 was written to God's people while in exile, promising them a deliverance from Babylon and reminding them of God's strength as Creator to save them from captivity and their own sins. At this time, Israel isn't strong enough to do anything to save itself, and God comes on the scene full of grace and promises of undeserved redemption.[11] I love the way one commentator puts it: God "insists that the judgment that befell them was not intended to destroy them and will have no power to do so (43:2). The only way of hope for these people is through the fires of judgment ... But it *is* the way of hope and not the way of destruction, as they feared."[12]

Sometimes the way of hope can look to us like the way of destruction. When we surrender to God in the process, admitting we can't save ourselves, He will pull us out of those pits and set our feet upon the rock of His sure foundation.

# 4

# THE SOLID FOOTING OF OBEDIENCE

*... and set my feet upon a rock,*
*making my steps secure.*

**PSALM 40:2b**

Before we begin, pray a prayer like this:

*Father God, open my mind so that I may understand the Scriptures, and my eyes that I may behold wondrous things in Your Word.*

In Session Three we touched on obedience, how it's better than sacrifice. In this session, we're going to talk more about obedience, what it is, what it means for us, and how it gives us solid footing.

Unfortunately obedience doesn't equal a trouble-free life. All you have to do is look through the Bible to see that some of the most obedient people had some of the hardest lives. Remember Joseph and Jeremiah? There is blessing in obedience, but blessing does not equal a pain-free existence.

Do you remember what *blessing* means? (We talked about it in Session Two, Day 4.)

*Blessing* means *to grant or bestow what is beneficial*, what will result in good, in the Romans 8:28 way.

## THE COMMAND AND THE SIN

In Genesis 2:16-17, God commanded Adam not to eat of "the tree of the knowledge of good and evil." If the man disobeyed God's command, he and Eve would die. The Hebrew in Genesis 2:17 repeats the word for die twice in a row, basically saying, "Dying you shall die," like when David said in Psalm 40:1, "Waiting I waited." This repetition is used to emphasize the certainty of the event occurring. The Hebrew word for "command" in Genesis 2:16 is *tsavah*. It means to appoint or command.

Adam was commanded not to eat of the tree. But of course, we know what happened. Adam and Eve disobeyed God's command, and literal death came into the world. Adam and Eve's bodies would wear out and die.

> **READ** Romans 5:12-14. What else came into the world when Adam and Eve disobeyed God?

God commands, and we disobey. Over and over and over again. Disobedience is our legacy—the blood in our veins comes all the way down from Adam. We inherited a fleshly, sinful nature from him.

But God knows this; He knows our poor and needy state, remember? It's why we need Jesus and why God sent Him. God knows we're prone to sin, to try to find our own way without Him, to think we know better when we get impatient or don't understand. He knows that all this dust we are made of is messy and in need of a good cleaning—an inside out cleaning that we are incapable of doing our own. But don't we like to try.

> **READ** Proverbs 6:16-19. What's first on this list of things God hates?

Why would God hate it when we exalt ourselves in our own eyes ("haughty eyes," v. 17)? (Hint: think about Genesis 3:1-6, or look up the word *exalt*.)

If we want to be obedient, we must first be humble. There's no obedience—the kind of heart obedience that God wants—without humility.

And what exactly is humility? It's becoming low—low before God and others.

What are we close to when we lower ourselves? Is humility difficult for you? Explain.

As we get low, we get closer to the ground, to the earth, the dirt from which we were formed.

We remember *dust to dust.*
We remember *we are the created.*
We remember *our breath is not our own.*
We remember *it is mercy that preserves our life.*

## *WHAT IS OBEDIENCE?*

**READ** Matthew 22:34-40. What's obedience, essentially?

To obey is to love God, to listen to what God tells us to do, and then, in humility, to do what He says. In obedience, we acknowledge that God loves us, has our best interests at heart, and He is much smarter than we are. In obedience, we are turning away from the idea that our plans or ideas are better than God's. And when we feel like we can't do it, we ask the Holy Spirit to intervene and give us the power and strength we need to do what we are called to do.

It's important to remember here that in our obedience we aren't earning our right standing before God. We can't obey God so perfectly that we "deserve" salvation. We obey out of an overflow of love and gratitude to God for Christ's sacrifice on our behalf.

Thinking about Matthew 22 again, how does God want us to love others?

When Jesus referred to "all the Law and the Prophets" (v. 40), He was alluding to the Old Testament. Basically, He was saying that everything God wants us to do as communicated in the Old Testament could fall under those two categories: love for God or love for neighbor. In fact, we see this sentiment echoed in the giving of the Ten Commandments in Exodus 20:1-17. The first four of the Ten Commandments have to do with loving God. The last six of the Ten Commandments give practical instruction as to how to love your neighbor.

READ John 14:15-27. How do we show that we love God?

READ 1 Corinthians 13:4-6, and fill in the blanks below.

Love Is:

Love Is Not:

Love means following his commandments, and his unifying commandment is that you conduct your lives in love. This is the first thing you heard, and nothing has changed.

**2 JOHN 1:6, THE MESSAGE**

We know that to love God means we keep His commands. How do we love one another?

**READ** John 14:25-27 again. What two things did Jesus say He was leaving with us on earth?

How does this give us peace and solid footing to obey God?

## HOW DOES OBEDIENCE GIVE US SOLID FOOTING?

There's blessing in keeping the Word of God. The love of God is perfected in us when we keep His Word. When we love God with our hearts, minds, and souls, we will do what He says, guarding His commandments.

What is solid footing? It's resting the full weight of our souls on the firm foundation of Christ, who makes our steps secure. It's trusting in God, our Rock. It's living by the power of the Holy Spirit, who enables our daily obedience and teaches us who God is, forming us more and more into His image.

Humility » Love » Obedience » Trust » Secure Ground

Look at the progression above. Which of these is difficult for you or hard to believe, if any? Explain.

When we obey God and keep His Word, He gives us an unshakable security and peace. It may be hard or confusing to obey at times, but the peace, the clear conscience, and the solid footing of following God as He leads will sustain us as a comfort to our souls.

In our obedience, God will give us new songs to sing. Additionally, others will see and put their trust in the Lord.

SESSION SIX:

# A NEW SONG

He put a new song in my mouth,
a song of praise to our God.

**PSALM 40:3a**

## GROUP GUIDE

**WARM THINGS UP**

Here are a few questions to begin your time.

> What from this week's personal study was particularly impactful for you?
>
> Think about the story of Joseph. What can we learn from his example? About how to handle suffering? About who God is?
>
> What about loving God can be difficult for you? What about loving others can be difficult for you?

**WATCH**

To view Session Six's teaching from Sarah Mae, download the optional video bundle at LifeWay.com/Psalm40.

**CREATE CONVERSATION**

> Share a little bit about how you came to be a Christ follower. Do you remember how it felt to encounter Jesus for the first time? Explain.
>
> Read Psalm 13 aloud together. Discuss any insights that stick out to you.
>
> Read Psalm 13:5 again. Ask each group member, as she is comfortable, to discuss what it would practically look like in her current life situation to trust in God's "steadfast love"?

Close your time with prayer, asking God to help you each see what song He has given you to sing in this season of life. Be especially mindful of those in the group who may be walking through a hard time, praying for God's presence to be near. Pray for God to protect each woman in your group from comparison. Ask Him to help you love one another well.

# *WHAT'S IN A SONG?*

## He put a new song in my mouth, a song of praise to our God.

### PSALM 40:3a

Before we begin, pray a prayer like this:

*Father God, open my mind so that I may understand the Scriptures, and my eyes that I may behold wondrous things in Your Word.*

I love music. To me, songs allow us to express our emotions and experiences in a unique way—to communicate our thoughts and feelings through tempo, beat, lyrics, and melody.

> If you could sum up the way your life is going right now in a song, what would that song be like? Wild, loud, upbeat? Slow, steady, soulful? Explain.

The way we live our lives, in a metaphorical sense, is the song we're singing. We've already discussed how the Psalms were poems and songs used in worship. Today, we're going to look at some of the other ways songs are used in the Bible and how God puts a new song in our mouths—a song of praise to Him. We find the first record of a song in the Bible in Exodus 15, though it's very likely that people were singing praises to God before this time.

**READ** Exodus 14:30 and Exodus 15:1-2. What's the first song in the Bible about?

The last recorded song in the Bible is found in Revelation 15.

**READ** Revelation 15:2-4. Who is singing (v. 2-3)?

What two songs are they singing (v. 3)?

In Revelation 15:3, the Bible says that the saints "who had conquered the beast" (v. 2) sang "the song of Moses" and something called "the song of the Lamb." Both are songs of victory—of deliverance. Moses and the people sang about deliverance from slavery in Egypt through the exodus. The overcoming saints in Revelation sang of the Lamb's power to save and how worthy He is of praise. They sang the song of Moses, about God's miraculous deliverance of His people, and the song of the Lamb, about Jesus defeating sin and death. It's so interesting to me too, that these saints weren't singing of their own victories in persevering to the end. Instead, they were praising God. One scholar says the use of these two songs seem to encompass God's redemptive acts through history—looking back to God's early deliverance of His people and looking forward to God's final and ultimate victory over sin and death, His final deliverance of His people.[1]

What happens between the two songs—the song of Moses and the victory song in Revelation? In between the first and last song are our songs—our lives—the songs of those in whom and through whom God is working so that others will see and fear and put their trust in Him.

## *WHAT'S OUR NEW SONG?*

**READ** Ephesians 2:11-22 again; we read it last session. As Gentiles, what new song has God given those of us who know Him?

The Jews sing praise to God because He chose them as His covenant people from the time of Abraham. We discussed this a little bit last week. The Bible calls those of us who are not ethnically Jewish Gentiles. Gentiles are now able to sing a new song, a song of victory and deliverance that God has chosen to include us as well, to adopt us as His children and heirs with Israel! We're saved from condemnation, washed and made clean, righteous, and set apart for God because of Jesus.

This is our new song, a song of praise to our God!

What was your old song? Before you had praise on your lips, what did you sing?

READ Psalm 30:11-12. What did God do with our mourning?

What did He clothe us in?

How long does David say in this psalm that he will give thanks to God?

How have you seen your times of mourning turn into dancing?

## JESUS SINGS

READ Matthew 26:26-30. What does this passage say that Jesus and His disciples did before they went out to the Mount of Olives?

What practice was Jesus instituting with His disciples in this passage?

This scene in Matthew 26, took place during the time of the Jewish Festival of Passover. The Passover feast commemorates part of God's deliverance of His people from Egyptian slavery. (See Exodus 12 for the full story.)

In the Jewish tradition, there is a group of psalms (Psalms 113–118), known as the Hallel (meaning, *praise*). The Jews recite, chant, or sing these psalms on major festive occasions,[2] including at the beginning of Passover.[3] The Hallel is also known as the "'The Egyptian Hallel,' because it was chanted in the temple whilst the Passover lambs were being slain."[4]

In the Jewish tradition, at the Passover meal the Hallel is split into two segments. Before the meal, the group will sing Psalms 113–114, psalms that commemo-rate God's past deliverance of His people—what He has done. Then, after the Passover meal is eaten, they will sing Psalm 115–118, psalms that praise God and celebrate His power and His future deliverance of His people, looking to the miracles that He will do in the coming days.[5]

It's very likely that Jesus, being Jewish, would have sung the Hallel at the Passover meal with His disciples.[6] Scholars think He and the disciples most likely sang the last round of Hallel, Psalms 115–118, before they went out to the Mount of Olives.[7]

Take a moment to skim the section headers in your Bible for Matthew 26–27. What happened in Jesus' life after this Passover meal in Matthew 26?

That's right, after this Passover meal and the institution of the Lord's Supper, Jesus prayed in the garden of Gethsemane, where He would be betrayed and arrested. Soon after, He would be falsely convicted and crucified. When He was enjoying the Passover meal with His disciples, Jesus knew exactly what was about to happen. Jesus knew the suffering and anguish that awaited Him.

It's beautiful to think that before going to the garden of Gethsemane Jesus sang Psalms 115–118—psalms that praised God for His power and goodness, songs that trusted and hoped in God's future deliverance, that pointed to Jesus' future victory on our behalf. Before going to the cross, Jesus chose to sing a song of hope, a song of trust, in God His Father. And as He sung, He knew the prophetic words were about to come true.

## *A MODEL FOR US*

In that Passover meal, Jesus instituted the Lord's Supper. He told us to practice it as His children. The Lord's Supper is a symbolic act of obedience in which we remember God's sacrifice on our behalf and we anticipate Jesus' future return for us, His children.[8] We look back at what God has done for us, and we praise Him. Then, we look forward in hope at what He will do on our behalf, and we praise Him. Sound familiar? God gives us this model of praise and thanksgiving in our lives. As we sing our songs, we can look back in thanks, tracing the thread of deliverance and what God has done for us; we can look forward with unshakable hope in the goodness and provision of our loving God.

Let's go ahead and start practicing this example now. Take a moment to fill in the blanks by crafting a poem, song, or prayer of praise to God.

Ways God has provided in the past:

Ways you can praise and trust God for the future:
(Hint: here you might include some of God's attributes.)

## 2

# *WHEN WE NEED A NEW SONG TODAY*

He put a new song in my mouth,
a song of praise to our God.

### PSALM 40:3a

Before we begin, pray a prayer like this:

*Father God, open my mind so that I may understand the Scriptures, and my eyes that I may behold wondrous things in Your Word.*

I'm so grateful for the new song God has given us in salvation. But as imperfect people living in this fallen world, where life can be really hard, we sometimes need new songs to trust God in every new day.

Remember the idea of honest church lyrics that I mentioned in Session One? It's the idea of singing lyrics in church that express what we're really feeling and what we really want to say to God, the hard and the easy, the gross and the beautiful—the idea of singing honestly without worrying about the approval of others. We see some of that in the Psalms, in David's honest pleas before the Lord, in the choruses He wrote to be sung by God's people.

If you're in a season of contentment and goodness in your life, then your new song right now is probably joyful and full of thanks. Praise God!

Some of us, though, are in a place right now where we feel abandoned by God. Some of us are pretty desperate for a new song right about now.

Maybe Job's words to God resonate with you:

> <sup>20</sup> I cry to you for help and you do not answer me;
> I stand, and you only look at me.
> <sup>21</sup> You have turned cruel to me;
> with the might of your hand you persecute me.

**JOB 30:20-21**

We're still clinging to that original, faithful new song we were given in our rebirth, when we went from dark to light, when we became new. But some days, things are feeling kind of old, kind of dim, and yeah, we may be moving our lips to the song, but ain't nothin' comin' out.

Whether we're in a happy season or a challenging season, we need to know how to come to God with our suffering and how to help those around us in theirs.

**READ** all of Psalm 13. What's the first word in verse 5?

What's the theme of the psalm before the "but"?

What's the theme of the psalm after the "but"?

Psalm 13 is a lament. Remember our discussion of *lament* in Session Two? It's a plea for God's deliverance. One scholar helps us understand the first piece of the psalm:

> The questions [the psalmist asked in Psalm 13:1-2] express the sense that God has withdrawn from the psalmist's present experience and has hidden himself. God's failure to appear and act leads to a fear of abandonment—that Yahweh has forgotten the psalmist. Such divine forgetfulness threatens to undo him, because to be known and remembered by God is to be in the relationship of blessing (as Ps. 1:6 clearly suggests).<sup>9</sup>

If it applies to you, and it's OK if it does, write down how you have felt abandoned by God.

A counselor of mine has told me, "It's OK that we will always have a little bit of sadness in our life regarding pain and loss. The goal isn't never to be sad; it's about getting to the point where the pain no longer consumes us or controls our perceptions of ourselves, others, God, and the world."

Looking at his current situation, it might be easy for the psalmist to despair. But, he puts his request for deliverance before the Lord again in verses 3-4. Nicholas Wolterstorff in his book *Lament for a Son* says, "Every lament is a love-song."[10] In bringing his pain and suffering to the Lord, the psalmist wasn't only acknowledging God's power to help him, but he was demonstrating an underlying belief that God cares for him.

Then, in verse 5, we come to the word "but"—a contrasting word, expressing the clear shift between questioning what appears to be God's abandonment and still believing God is loving and good. David highlighted the paradox of suffering in the life of God's children—the tension between what may feel like God's abandonment and God's trustworthy steadfast love, a salvation worth rejoicing in, and the bountiful way He deals with us.

One scholar has called Psalm 13 "Dark and Dawn."[11] In verses 1-4, we see the dark as the psalmist acknowledged the reality of his desperate situation and pain. Then, in verse 5, the first rays of sun broke through. As the psalmist reminded himself of the truth of God's goodness and character, He committed to moving forward in trust and surrender. "Despite his loneliness, the psalmist's faith is unshaken. Faith knows that God will have the last word. And faith expects it to be a good word. God gives us our song back and restores the joy of our salvation."[12]

Now look up the word *bountiful,* and write its definition below.

Write down a few ways God has dealt bountifully with you.

For those of us in a season of pain, loss, or hardship, our new songs today, the ones we need to release from our mouths, are perhaps one of paradox.

Maybe your song has lyrics like this:

*Why, God, would you let me have a miscarriage?*
*Why would you allow my dad to leave my mom?*
*Why would you give me this struggle I can't break free of?*
*Why would you allow that awful thing to happen?*
*Why have you turned your face from me in this pain?*
*I'm hurt and confused, and I feel like you left me here alone.*

**But**, *I know You love me and that You are good. I have settled it in my heart. I will rejoice in Your salvation and I will sing to You because I have seen Your work in my life, and I know You'll do it again.*

Take a few minutes and write your own version of Psalm 13 below:

Why God:

Consider and answer me:

But,

God may never explain the whys of all of the hard things in our lives. We may never get the full picture. But, with eyes of faith we can know God has the last word. And we can, by faith expect "it to be a good word."[13]

## A NEW SONG

You may be thinking, this is all great theoretically, but if I'm having a hard time, what do I practically do? If you want a new song, seek God's face.

READ Psalm 27:8, and write it below in your own words.

God wants us to seek His face. That's clear. But what does it mean to seek His face?

Look up the word *seek*, and write the definition below.

In Psalm 27:8, the psalmist was "expressing the heartfelt desire to come into the presence of Yahweh."[14] To seek God's face "involves complete devotion to God in the same sense as turning toward Him."[15] It's usually within the context of worship. Here the psalmist is also asking God not to hide His face from the psalmist.[16] To seek God's face is to seek Him up close, to be intimately acquainted with Him, to look for, to beg for, to earnestly desire to know Him more in relationship.

People often talk about seeking God's face in contrast to seeking His hand, in other words, wanting God's presence in relationship with us versus wanting what God can give us. In our relationships, we would much rather be friends with people who simply enjoy us as people than those who are looking for what they can get from us or what they can get out of our relationships. Right? The trick is, when we seek God's face and have the joy of His presence, we get all that we need. And, what's more, we get God! His presence is the ultimate gift.

As we close today, think about your time with God. Do you most often seek His face or His hand? What keeps you from seeking His face? Explain. Feel free to answer this question in your journal.

# 3

# *PRAISE HIM!*

He put a new song in my mouth,
a song of praise to our God.

**PSALM 40:3a**

Before we begin, pray a prayer like this:

*Father God, open my mind so that I may understand the Scriptures, and my eyes that I may behold wondrous things in Your Word.*

As we spend more time with God, seeking His face and getting to know Him, we're going to learn more and more how wonderfully worthy of praise He is. Over and over in the Bible, God commands us to praise Him. The word *praise* is used more than one hundred times just in the Psalms.

What does the word *praise* mean? When we praise God, we, as humans, are responding to God's revelation of Himself to us. In praise, we're proclaiming God's "merit or worth." Praise isn't just something relegated to worship services; in fact it's associated with our everyday lives. In our daily busyness of going to work, loving our families, and walking through the checkout line, we can praise God; we can highlight His greatness and worth. You won't be surprised to hear this, I'm sure, but the idea of true praise is associated with a posture of the heart and not how polished or put together a person may look on the outside.[17]

The word David used for "praise" in Psalm 40:3 means what you would typically associate with worship or praise—to adore, often with song, from a "deep place."[18] The word comes from the Hebrew word *Halel* meaning literally, to shine. (This *Halel* is a bit different than the *Hallel* that we discussed earlier, but both words carry a similar idea of praise.) When we praise God, we're giving glory to Him. His light within us shines back to Him. It's as if we're saying, *Look! Look at God, at who God is and what He does!*

## WHY SHOULD WE SING PRAISES?

**READ** Psalm 33. Scholars sometimes break this Psalm into four parts. See if you can identify and record each below. I've filled in the first one for you.

Part 1: *Verses 1-3, a call to praise and worship God*

Part 2:

Part 3:

Part 4:

## WE PRAISE THE LORD BECAUSE HE IS GREAT.

The truth of the first "why" of praise is an undeniable fact: we praise God because He deserves it, and He tells us to praise Him. Because God is so different from us—so fully incomprehensible—His mystery can be frustrating and scary sometimes, especially in seasons of hardship and pain. But, ultimately the fact that God is higher than us, that we can't wrap our minds around the entirety of who He is, is a good thing! We wouldn't want to worship a God who we could completely understand. If we could fully understand Him, then we'd be on His same level and He wouldn't be God.

As God reveals different aspects of His character to us and as we come to understand more and more of what He has done for us as His children, we will discover reason after reason to praise Him. The old hymn "Come, Ye Sinners, Poor and Needy" says God has "ten thousand charms."[19] I love to think of God that way. There are always more beautiful aspects of His character and love for us to discover. We'll never come to the end of who He is. And, when He shows us more of who He is through His Word and prayer, we respond to that revelation with praise and gratitude.

## WE PRAISE GOD BECAUSE IT HELPS US.

God made us. He knows how we were created to flourish and thrive. He commands us to praise Him because He knows the best thing for us is to prize Him as the joy and delight of our hearts. When our relationship with God is prioritized first and we're placing the full weight of not only our eternal security but our emotional and spiritual security here and now on God, we typically give the people in our lives more freedom. And that leads to healthier and more loving relationships and more internal security.

Praising God also helps us because it reminds us of the truth of His Word, and gives us a way to turn His gospel truths over and over in our hearts and minds. Think back to the "but" we discussed in Psalm 13 and how that contrasting word signifies a shift in the psalmist's language and his heart and mind. Over and over again in the psalms, we see men grappling with devastating loss, pain, and fear, only to turn the corner with "but." Then we see God's Word walk them back from the edge of despair. Praising God helps anchor us in the truths of His character and His steadfast love for us. It reminds us that He holds onto us during the good and the bad days. Praising God stirs our hearts up to joy so we can walk in hope-filled assurance of who God is. It's a reminder that God isn't done with us yet. Though things may look grim now, His truth and Word will hold us until eternity. God has good plans for us still.

## WE PRAISE GOD TO MAKE MUCH OF HIM TO OTHERS.

We praise God and shine a light on Him, giving Him glory so that others will see how great He is. We tell of His goodness to other believers to encourage them, to strengthen their hope and faith in Him. (We'll talk more about praising God in the congregation in the next session.) We tell of His goodness to those who do not yet know God, so that they can see how all-satisfying a relationship with Him is, so that they will want to know Him too.

> Think about your typical practice of praise. After our discussion of the "why" of praise, is there anything you should change? Stop doing? Start doing? Discuss.

# WHEN SHOULD WE SING PRAISES?

When should we sing, shining a light on God and giving Him glory? Hebrews 13:15 says, "let us continually offer up a sacrifice of praise to God." And the Bible gives us examples of people praising God in a variety of circumstances. People praised God for victory in battle, while they were sitting in a jail cell, and in big moments of Israel's history, like the dedication of the temple in Jerusalem (2 Chron. 5). God wants us to sing praises to Him all the time, in good and bad circumstances.

Let's look at another example of praises being offered in Scripture and a unique word that's used for praise.

> **READ** Exodus 15:2, and write it out below.

Exodus 15, if you remember, was the first song recorded in the Bible. It's a song of deliverance, celebrating how God miraculously saved His people from Egyptian slavery.

> In Exodus 15:2 that you wrote above, circle the word *praise*.

In the original Hebrew language, the word used here for *praise* is a bit different than we're accustomed to. One of the meanings of the word used for *praise* here is *to beautify.*

> Consider this for a moment. How do you think our exaltation of God makes Him beautiful?

Our last Scripture passage for this session is Mary's tender praise in Luke 1.

**READ** Luke 1 below. Circle, underline, and highlight anything that stands out to you or that you find particularly beautiful.

<sup>30</sup> And the angel said to her, "Do not be afraid, Mary, for you have found favor with God. <sup>31</sup> And behold, you will conceive in your womb and bear a son, and you shall call his name Jesus. <sup>32</sup> He will be great and will be called the Son of the Most High. And the Lord God will give to him the throne of his father David ...
<sup>46</sup> And Mary said, "My soul magnifies the Lord,
<sup>47</sup> and my spirit rejoices in God my Savior,
<sup>48</sup> for he has looked on the humble estate of his servant.
For behold, from now on all generations will call me blessed;
<sup>49</sup> for he who is mighty has done great things
for me, and holy is his name.
<sup>50</sup> And his mercy is for those who fear him
from generation to generation.
<sup>51</sup> He has shown strength with his arm; he has scattered
the proud in the thoughts of their hearts;
<sup>52</sup> he has brought down the mighty from their thrones
and exalted those of humble estate;
<sup>53</sup> he has filled the hungry with good things,
and the rich he has sent away empty.
<sup>54</sup> He has helped his servant Israel,
in remembrance of his mercy,
<sup>55</sup> as he spoke to our fathers,
to Abraham and to his offspring forever."

**LUKE 1:30-32,46-55**

What about Mary's praise in this passage stands out to you? Why?

## 4

# FOR THE CONGREGATION

He put a new song in my mouth,
a song of praise to our God.

**PSALM 40:3a**

Before we begin, pray a prayer like this:

*Father God, open my mind so that I may understand the Scriptures, and my eyes that I may behold wondrous things in Your Word.*

As you know, I love songs. And there's something about singing worship songs together in church that's so encouraging. In moments of joy, we as a faith family are able to celebrate God's goodness together. In moments of doubt or suffering, when we struggle to muster words of praise, hearing the men and women around us confidently sing of God's kindness and love is a balm to the soul. It's almost as if they're singing over us when we can't sing God's truth for ourselves. This tangible manifestation of God's grace to us through our brothers and sisters reminds us of who God is and renews our hope and strength.

How would you describe your faith family? Take a few minutes to list the things that you love about your church.

**READ** Psalm 40:9-10 written out for you below. Underline everywhere you see the words "I have" and "I have not." Now circle the word that follows the underlined words.

> ⁹ I have told the glad news of deliverance
> in the great congregation;
> behold, I have not restrained my lips,
> as you know, O LORD.
> ¹⁰ I have not hidden your deliverance within my heart;
> I have spoken of your faithfulness and your salvation;
> I have not concealed your steadfast love and your faithfulness
> from the great congregation.

### PSALM 40:9-10

Write the underlined words and the circled words below. I've gotten you started by listing the first one below.

*I have told.*

Where is all this telling and not restraining of the lips happening?

**READ** the following Scriptures. Beside each reference, list what the psalmist was doing "in the congregation."

Psalm 22:25

Psalm 35:18

Psalm 111:1

Now let's skip back a bit. God has an "honest church song" for the congregation as well, maybe a little different than the ones we've been discussing up to now.

**READ** Deuteronomy 31:19-22. What did God tell Moses to do in verse 19?

According to the passage, why does God tell Moses to do this?

The whole song the people of Israel had to learn, all forty-three verses, is found in Deuteronomy 32. Before we dive into chapter 32, we need to discuss a bit of the larger context of this passage. At this time in history, Moses—who had led the Israelites for many years, including in the exodus out of Egypt—was getting older. God had told Moses to pass the leadership of His people over to Joshua. This song in chapter 32 is one of the last addresses that Moses made to God's people; he also blessed the people in chapter 33 before he died in chapter 34. In this song, we find the words of a loving leader who wanted to make sure the people he had cared for over many years were prepared to follow God, even after he was no longer there to lead them.

**READ** Deuteronomy 32. I know it's long, but it will help in our discussion to get a sense of the entire song.

**READ** verse 2. How did God want His words to fall on the people?

I love the imagery used in verse 2. God was comparing His people to thirsty plants that soak up the rain. He was saying He hoped their hearts would be tender and receptive to the words He was about to speak to them through Moses.

**READ** verses 5-6 and 16-17. How had the people dealt with God?

**READ** verses 10-12. How did God care for His people?


**READ** verses 18-20. How did God respond to the people?


**READ** verse 36. When would God vindicate His people?


Quick aside here. It fuels my worship to understand that though God was disappointed and angry at Israel's failure to honor Him, He affirmed in verse 36 that He would still be faithful to the promises He had made to them.

**READ** verses 44-47. What three things did Moses tell the people to do?


Write verse 47 below.


As I said earlier, this "honest church song" is a little different from the others that we've been discussing. How does it strike you that this type of song was also presented to the church body? How would you describe its tone?


Why do you think it's important that the whole congregation, all the people, learn this song together? What benefit might it have?


Deuteronomy 32 is an indictment of Israel's faithlessness before God and a call to repent, to turn back to God, and to tell the next generation of God's goodness and care for Israel. We don't often sing honest church songs about the pain and despair of our hearts. Neither do we sing songs about our corporate sin and rebellion.

**READ** Galatians 5:9. Do you have any idea what the words "lump" or "batch" might be referring to in this passage?

Galatians 5 is a discussion of a false gospel that had been creeping into the early church. Paul not only wrote the church at Galatia to help them correct the theological error, but he also reminded them of how their beliefs affected one another within the church. We don't often like to think of it, but as members of the same church, we're inextricably linked in our holiness and sin. The health of each member of our church affects all of the other members. Part of loving our brothers and sisters in church is not only fighting for our own joy and spiritual health, but fighting for the holiness, flourishing, and spiritual health of our faith family members as well.

We need each other. We aren't meant to be loners, or to go it alone. And when we get together with the congregation of believers, we're to be honest with one another, so that we can encourage, sharpen, and spur each other on to keep going.

We need to tell each other our stories, our Psalm 40 stories, because in our telling, in the unrestrainedness of our lips, we remind each other of and shine a light on God's faithfulness, His salvation, and His steadfast love.

For the remainder of this session, write a letter to the other women in this study. Tell them a Psalm 40 story from your life. It can be a big, life-changing kind of story, or a small, sweet story of how you've seen God working in or around your life recently.

At the next study, if you feel comfortable, read your letter to the women in your group.

SESSION SEVEN:

# PEOPLE WILL SEE

Many will see and fear,
and put their trust in the LORD.

**PSALM 40:3b**

# GROUP GUIDE

## WARM THINGS UP

Here are a few questions to begin your time.

> Share with the group the type of song you chose to describe your current life situation in Day 1 of last session's personal study. Explain why you chose what you did.

> Share with the group one reason why you've praised God in the past week.

> In your opinion, does your church have a culture of open and honest communication? Discuss.

> How do you fight for the holiness and joy of the other women in your group? How do others fight for your holiness and joy?

## WATCH

To view Session Seven's teaching from Sarah Mae, download the optional video bundle at LifeWay.com/Psalm40.

## CREATE CONVERSATION

> How did you hear about Jesus for the first time?

> In the video, Sarah Mae says, "Our stories are meant to give glory to God; they are not our own." Do you agree or disagree? Discuss it with one another.

> Is there a part of your story that God could use to encourage others? If you feel comfortable, share it with the women in your group. (Maybe it's the Psalm 40 story that you recorded at the end of last session.)

Close your time with prayer, asking God to help you each see what part of your story might be an encouragement to others—a story that could bring glory to God. Consider who might need to hear that story this week. And, tell it to them!

# 1

# *FEAR AND TRUST FOR THE BELIEVER*

## Many will see and fear, and put their trust in the LORD.

### PSALM 40:3b

Before we begin, pray a prayer like this:

*Father God, open my mind so that I may understand the Scriptures, and my eyes that I may behold wondrous things in Your Word.*

There's a connection between fear and trust, and in this session, we're going to work out that connection, focusing specifically on what it means to fear the Lord. We need a clear picture of what it means to fear the Lord so we don't have an unhealthy view.

I like to think of it this way: as Christians, because we have Jesus' righteousness accredited to us, we're no longer afraid of God's wrath in judgment. As children of God, the Bible instructs us to fear the Lord in the sense of having a loyal love and allegiance to Him and His instructions for our lives. Put another way, "knowing that God's wrath has been satisfied in Christ relieves the believer from the fear of condemnation but not from accountability to a holy God."[1] In other words, as followers of Jesus, we're eternally safe from condemnation. We're also bound in covenant love with God, to honor and follow Him. That includes humbly submitting our lives to Him—our choices, attitudes, and the way we act.[2] God is holy. We don't want to ever take advantage of His grace toward us.

We no longer need to fear God's condemnation, but we must maintain a righteous fear of the Lord. If we believe Jesus, then we can walk in the fear of the Lord and the comfort of the Holy Spirit in a healthy way.

Would you say that you fear the Lord? Why or why not?

Is it hard for you to submit your choices, behaviors, and attitudes to God? Is one most difficult for you? Explain.

## DEFINITIONS:

Trust – (Hebrew – batach) a primitive root; properly, to hide for refuge; ... figuratively, to trust, be confident or sure: — be bold (confident, secure, sure), careless (one, woman), put confidence, (make to) hope, (put, make to) trust.[3]

Fear – (Hebrew – yare) to fear; morally to revere; causatively to frighten: — affright, be (make) afraid, dread.[4]

READ Genesis 3:10, the first mention of fearing God in the Bible. Why was Adam afraid (yare)? What did he do in response?

How did Adam know he was naked? Look at Genesis 3:11b.

Adam was afraid because, in his nakedness, his sin was exposed. There was a consequence to the broken trust between Adam and Eve and their disobedience of God's command, a punishment: death. Fear and punishment wrapped up together. Jesus came to rescue us from the fear that Adam and Eve brought into the human race.

**READ** 1 John 4:7-18. What casts out fear?

If you fear, what have you not been perfected in? How is love perfected in us?

This passage in 1 John is about the life-giving love of God. God is the only source of love. He invented love. God, in loving us, shows us what love is. Then He commanded us to love one another and mirror His character to the people around us. Our fear abates as we come to understand the greatness of God's love for us.

According to this passage, we can understand the magnitude of God's love for us in several ways:

- the immeasurable worth of the gift God gave us in the sacrifice of Jesus on the cross;

- the motivation for Jesus' mission on earth—that we could have life through Him;

- our unworthy condition and earthy state when Jesus came to redeem us; and

- the great sacrifice and pain through which our redemption was purchased.[5]

First John 4:16 tells us that the assurance of our eternal salvation can be "a settled state of mind and heart"[6] that's dependent upon faith in God's character and the finished work of Jesus. This passage reminds us that God's "perfect love casts out fear" of eternal judgment (v. 18). I don't know about you, but that's such good news to me  Friend, if you aren't sure whether or not you've given your life to God, and whether or not eternal salvation is yours, visit "Becoming a Christian" (p. 184) in the back of the book for more information on how you can become a follower of Jesus.

READ Romans 8:38-39, and write down all the things that *can* separate us from the love of God in Christ Jesus.

Now write down all the things that *can't* separate us from the love of God in Christ Jesus according to Romans 8:38-39.

1.

2.

3.

4.

5.

6.

7.

8.

9.

10.

Those of us who call Jesus our Lord and have submitted our lives to Him will pass from death to eternal life with the righteousness of Christ accredited to us. We'll be safe from eternal judgment and condemnation, secure in our Father's love.

The fear of the Lord for believers isn't one of fearing punishment. Our punishment for sin has already been taken by Jesus. Jesus has given us credit before God for the righteous life He lived here on earth. Without fearing punishment, how does a believer then walk in the fear of the Lord today?

Many of the principles found in the Old Testament that address fearing the Lord are still true for us today.

**READ** Proverbs 1:7. Write it below.

Why do you think fearing God is the beginning of all knowledge?

Proverbs is often referred to as wisdom literature in the Bible. Proverbs 1:7 represents a central truth from the Book of Proverbs from which everything else flows, "the quest for wisdom begins with the fear of the Lord."[7] The difference between knowledge and wisdom as described in the Book of Proverbs is that knowledge deals with "correct understanding of the world and oneself as creatures of the magnificent and loving God."[8] Wisdom "is the acquired skill of applying that knowledge rightly."[9] So reverence of God, righteous fear of Him, is the foundation for all the spiritual knowledge and wisdom we can gain, and it helps us see the world rightly. And as we see the world rightly, God will teach us how to use that knowledge the best possible way in the world He made. Remember last week when we discussed the way praise helps us to prioritize our relationship with God above all else? The fear of the Lord has a similar effect.

Deuteronomy 6:24 says, "And the LORD commanded us to do all these statutes, to fear the LORD our God, for our good always, that he might preserve us alive, as we are this day." And Proverbs 10:27a says, "The fear of the LORD prolongs life." In this Proverbs passage, God's not promising that if you fear the Lord you're going to absolutely live to be 100 years old. This proverb provides a general guiding principle for life, as many of the proverbs do. Ultimately, the Bible consistently tells us that fearing God and pursuing wisdom are to our benefit.

**READ** Psalm 25:14. Think about why a friendship with God, or secret council with God, would be forged through the fear of Him? Ponder it, and write your thoughts below.

**READ** Proverbs 16:6. What does fearing the Lord help us to do?

**READ** Proverbs 3:11-12. If you're honest, how do you usually react when someone corrects you or questions you? Explain.

Discipline, as used in the New Testament, trains us up to reach our full maturity in Christ. It often involves suffering, because suffering strips away everything and reveals what's in our hearts. I love how Dave Furman puts it: "your circumstances don't create what's in your heart; your situation is simply the stage on which the heart's condition is revealed."[10]

**READ** Romans 2:4 and Galatians 6:1. What's the goal of reproof (the exposure of our sin) and the spirit behind it?

Reproof, as used in the New Testament, is to convince someone with solid, compelling evidence, especially "to expose" or "by conviction to bring to the light."[11] Reproof specifically helps us stay on the path of life. If we fear God, we'll cooperate with God as He exposes our sin, in love, to correct us.

Has fearing the Lord ever led you to turn away from evil? If so, explain below.

How does fearing the Lord as a believer lead to trusting Him?

As we fear God, we submit to His kind correction and we grow to look more like Him, loving others and pointing them to Christ. We'll talk more about that tomorrow.

## 2

# *WHAT DO PEOPLE SEE AND HEAR?*

### Many will see and fear,
### and put their trust in the LORD.

### PSALM 40:3b

Before we begin, pray a prayer like this:

*Father God, open my mind so that I may understand the Scriptures, and my eyes that I may behold wondrous things in Your Word.*

Take a look above at Psalm 40:3.

*Who* will see and fear and trust?

Our life stories, life change, and life offerings are for those who don't know the Lord and for those who do. God weaves stories out of our lives so others will put their faith in the Lord for salvation, but they are also for those who know the Lord and have perhaps grown weary, complacent, or unsure—for those who are barely holding on. David's song is for anyone who needs to know or remember who God is—our songs and stories are too.

## *WHEN PEOPLE LOOK AT YOUR LIFE, WHAT DO THEY SEE AND HEAR?*

Take a few minutes, and using your imagination, step outside of yourself and try to look at your life objectively. What do you observe? (You are simply observing, truth-telling, in a non-judgmental way. There are no rules for exactly how this should look. Just be curious about the life you see before you.) In the space below, write what you see.

When I observe _____'s (your name) life, I see …

When you look at David's life, what do you see? Think back to our earlier study.

List below what you see in the lives of each Bible figure or group.

Adam and Eve

Abraham and Sarah

Hagar

Jacob

Jacob's sons

The Israelites in the desert

When I consider the lives of these ancient Near Eastern people, I see lives full of humanity. I see people trying to figure out how to live on this fallen earth in the midst of complicated hearts that hold sin and wounds and pain, people trying to see and follow and trust God, people who just keep failing.

**READ** the verse from Numbers below.

> But if you sin unintentionally, and do not
> observe all these commandments …
>
> **NUMBERS 15:22**

What word comes after "But"? Circle it.

Now rewrite this verse below but replace "you" with "I."

God knows you will fail at times—sometimes unintentionally and sometimes intentionally. You won't have it all together this side of glory, so take some comfort in the fact that it's human to fail. You cannot and will not be perfect on this earth. But, we still try!

**READ** Psalm 73:26. Who is our strength and our portion when we fail?

What does all this failing and humanity have to do with what people see? It has to do with living honestly. It's in the honesty of our lives, the relatedness of humanity, that when God works, people see. But in order to live honest lives, we need to be willing to live humble lives. In the humility comes the healing, and in the healing comes the hope, and in the hope comes the honesty that gives glory to God. We know we can be honest because we have experienced the healing and have the hope that only the gospel offers; we can remember and know that God is faithful.

**READ** Psalm 32. What happens when we keep silent about our sin?

What happens when we acknowledge our sin to God?

What surrounds us when we trust the Lord?

This psalm celebrates the freedom that comes with confession of sin and God's forgiveness. Giving thanks for God's goodness, this psalm also "[encourages] the reader not to resist the guidance of Yahweh but to trust fully in him."[12] After the psalmist confessed his sin, he enjoyed a clear conscience. The end of the psalm shows some of the many benefits of being God's children—including being enveloped by God's grace.

What does trusting the Lord have to do with being honest about our sin?


What keeps us from being honest about our sin before God?
(See Gen. 3:10.)


The bondage of fear and shame is fierce. When we're afraid to come clean, to be honest about our wounds and weaknesses, secrets and sin, we're choosing to go back to the chains Jesus released us from.

When we're honest with God, we can begin to get help that leads to healing and freedom, and then that freedom becomes contagious. We want to tell people, "One thing I do know, that though I was blind, now I see" (John 9:25).

And the redemption rhythm keeps on.

Honest with God » Experience God's Grace with
Healing and Freedom from the Bonds of Fear » Honest
with Others » Shared Humanity » Honest with God

This is the Psalm 40 mandate—the gospel call to the world and to each other.

When we live true, we let what God has done and is doing in our lives shine through us, giving glory to Him. There is life change.

Keep your conduct among the Gentiles [unbelievers] honorable,
so that when they speak against you as evildoers, they may see
your good deeds and glorify God on the day of visitation.

## 1 PETER 2:12

The word "honorable" here means "beautiful" or "attractively good; good that inspires (motivates) others to embrace what is lovely."[13]

Isn't it beautiful and inspiring when we see someone's life change because of how God has worked? I love a good, honest, miraculous "God story." Don't you?

The thing about our stories is that we're always in the middle of one. God is always working and leading, offering healing and freedom for our good and His glory and the good of the church. There will always tangles in our hearts—wounds and sin and fear all twisted up—needing to be untangled until we step out of these bodies and into glory. The good news is, the more we submit to the untangling, to the work of God in making us look more like Him, the freer we become, maturing, and living spiritually and emotionally healthier lives. The freer and healthier we become, the better we love.

More on the inspiration of our beautiful God story lives in the next session!

How did God speak to you today?

What's your response to Him?

# 3

# *PIT AND PRAISE,*
# *BLOOD AND BEAUTY*

### Many will see and fear,
### and put their trust in the LORD.

#### PSALM 40:3b

Before we begin, pray a prayer like this:

*Father God, open my mind so that I may understand the Scriptures, and my eyes that I may behold wondrous things in Your Word.*

What will people see that will make them fear and put their trust in the Lord?

Have you ever seen something in someone's life that caused you to stand in awe of the Lord and trust Him more? If so, what was it?

I can recall several instances in my life when I saw or heard something that caused an awe in me, a reverence, that compelled me to believe and trust in God. Sometimes, even before I became a Christian, the awe was so overwhelming that it felt as though the air got sucked right out of my lungs and my heart prostrated before the God I didn't even yet know.

It is this seeing and hearing that causes a compelling in others, and this is why we don't hide our light under a bushel.

**READ** Matthew 5:14-16. Why do we let our light shine before others?

What is this good work? Let's look at the meaning of the word "good" here, because it's quite significant.

The Greek word for "good" in Matthew 5:16 is *kalos*. We talked about it some in Day 2. In this context it means "beautiful, as an outward sign of the inward good, noble, honorable character; good, worthy, honorable, noble, and seen to be so."[14]

Your beautiful life, the life God has made beautiful because of Jesus, will inspire others to embrace Him if you're willing to share it. Share your life and your story and your song and let the pit and the praise be seen. Let people see how God has redeemed and rescued you and takes care of you each day.

## PIT AND PRAISE, BLOOD AND BEAUTY

**READ** Exodus 28:1-2. In this passage, God told Moses to make Aaron and Aaron's sons priests. Aaron, who was a high priest, was to have holy garments made for him. What was the purpose of these garments for Aaron?

One of the priest's jobs was to intercede for the people by making sacrifices for their sins, specifically, by slaughtering an animal and shedding its blood. Some of this will probably sound familiar from our earlier discussion of the sacrificial system. With the shedding of blood, there's atonement for the sins of the people.

It was a messy job. Bloody. Ugly. And yet, God used the words "glory" and "beauty" to describe Aaron's holy garments (v. 2).

Aaron, who was a high priest (able to enter the holy of holies) and a slaughterer of sacrificial animals, was to wear something beautiful. What a juxtaposition of blood and beauty.

> Why do you think God would have Aaron wear something beautiful in order to do something so seemingly ugly?

Scholars have several different ideas as to why God specified that Aaron's garments should be "for glory and for beauty" (v. 2). Some believe that the garments were made specifically to elevate the office and the role of the priest. Such nice clothes would have visually set Aaron apart as special to God in the eyes of the people, just as the role that he served in mediating between the people and God was special.[15] Others believe that these garments were made of specific materials, similar to the specifications for the building of the tabernacle, to remind the people of the holiness of the place in which the priests ministered and the glory of God, who the priests served.[16] Lastly, some scholars believe these garments were meant to look almost royal. At this time, Israel didn't have a human king; God was their ruler. The high priest was effectively the leader of the people, God's appointed leader, for the purposes of worship. These clothes were meant to show his prominent position.[17]

There's a really beautiful tie in to the priesthood that I want us to see next.

> Let's turn to Hebrews to see what we can find out.

> **READ** Hebrews 2:14-15. What did God partake of? Why?

**READ** Hebrews 2:17. Who was Jesus made like in every way?


Write Hebrews 2:17 below, and underline the part of the passage that answers why Jesus was like man in every way.


**READ** Romans 8:31-34. We really only need to read verse 34 for this question, but verses 31-33 are so beautiful, I couldn't help myself!

Focus on verse 34. What is Jesus doing now for us?


Think a moment about the fact that Jesus is interceding for you before God the Father. Journal your thoughts below. Are you blown away by this? Upset by it? Explain.


God, in sending Jesus, enclosed Himself in flesh and blood in order to defeat the power of sin and death. He came down in love to relate to us in order to save us, to become our merciful and faithful High Priest. Jesus had to become fully man—like us in every respect, except Jesus was and is sinless—to represent believers as our High Priest.

Jesus is the offerer and the offering.

He took what was ugly and, by His love, surrendered His life so that we could be covered by His righteousness in God's eyes. He wrapped Himself in flesh so that we could have His indwelling Spirit. Jesus is God with us.

Jesus partook in our flesh and blood as a man, and He continues to serve us today as our great High Priest, who intercedes on our behalf. And today the Holy Spirit continues to partake in our flesh and blood by living in us.

Through the working of the Holy Spirit and because of Jesus' blood, God takes all the ugly and makes it beautiful. Blood and beauty. Pit and praise. Many will see and fear and put their trust in the Lord.

This, the pit to the praise, the ugly to the beautiful, this is the light God wants you to shine—showing the fruit in your life in keeping with repentance, helping God's children see His will for them, and displaying the joy of the redemption He's wrought and keeps cultivating in your life—your beautiful story that is God's story of love for you and for the world.

Will you show and tell?

How did God speak to you today?

What's your response to Him?

## 4

# *YOUR STORY, YOUR TURN*

## Many will see and fear,
## and put their trust in the LORD.

### PSALM 40:3b

Before we begin, pray a prayer like this:

*Father God, open my mind so that I may understand the Scriptures, and my eyes that I may behold wondrous things in Your Word.*

On our last day of study—*can you believe it's the last day?*—let's do a bit of self-reflection.

What's your story or your song?

Are you ready for a new one?

What has God done for you and through you?

How did God do it?


How is God doing it, right now?


What does the Bible say God will do if you trust Him?


When we opened this study together, I asked, "What would happen if people knew?" What would happen if we shared our secrets, our hidden pain, our unhealed wounds, our doubts, and our sin? What if we were ready to deal with our emotional and spiritual junk? Could we be secure enough in the love and security and identity of Christ to be willing to come out from hiding and stand in truth in trust? Could we be willing to get help in faith? Maybe counseling or honest conversations with a friend. Maybe confession to a spouse. Maybe finally letting go of pretense before the Lord and letting Him into what's really going on in our hearts and minds? What if we could trust Him enough to go through the pain of processing the hurt to get to the peace—the peace He alone gives when we trust Him in the suffering, knowing that He is with us and sanctifying us every step of the way? No suffering is in vain. God's love is always working.

Are you ready to take the next vulnerable step that God is calling you to take? If so, what's that vulnerable next step for you? If no, explain why not.

What fear, if any, are you still holding onto when it comes to obeying God in facing your pain, telling the truth, exposing your sin, or being vulnerable?

Are you willing to trust God, even in the fear, to work good through your willingness to obey in what He's calling you to do or believe?

**READ** Psalm 56:3. Does this verse say "if" or "when"?

Do you find comfort in the fact that the biblical accounts allow for honesty?

In Psalm 56, the psalmist was up against some very real threats. But, in his fear and panic, he chose to turn to trust in God. I really like how one commentator says it:

> In spite of his fear, the poet puts his trust in God, and that leads him from fear to confidence. While his enemies might be dangerous, he knows that they are no match for God.[18]

We can do the same thing. Sometimes scary things happen to us. But we can choose to add a "but" to our story (remember Psalm 13?) and turn away from fear to trust God's power and kindness instead.

When you decide to obey God with something that feels scary or nerve-wracking or vulnerable, consider writing Psalm 56:3 on your hand or in a place you will you see it to encourage you as you do the thing you're afraid to do.

**READ** Psalm 118:6-7. Who is with you? What is He called?

The Hebrew word here that's used for "helper" in verse 7 has the sense of surrounding someone to "protect or aid."[19] God surrounds us with His love and protection when we cry out to Him for help. The Lord is on our side; what can men do to us?

Sometimes we need to remind ourselves to have courage, and this verse is a call to do that, to have courage and to remember who is with you and helping you as you obey.

> On the previous page, I asked you to identify the next step of obedience that God is asking you to take. Some of us may have struggled to come up with a next step. If that's you, I'm including some suggestions for you below. If you have your own steps of obedience, that's great. Use your own ideas or the prompts below. Pick one or more to do this week, perhaps even today.
>
> □ Call a counselor.
> □ Call a friend who needs a safe friend to talk to. Be that safe friend.
> □ Call a friend and share what you're struggling with.
> □ Confess a sin to God.
> □ Come clean with your husband about what's on your heart.
> □ Cry out to God in truth.
> □ Consult a doctor, a physician, or a mental health professional.
> □ Claim a promise from God.
> □ Cuddle up with your child and tell your child you're sorry. Ask your child to forgive you.
> □ Record your story. (Write it. Make an audio or video recording of it. Sing it. Draw it.)
> □ Confront your fear by asking God to show you the root of the fear and how you can be free of it. Wait. Listen. Obey as He leads.
> □ Courageously share your story with someone who will benefit from it.

6 Don't fret or worry. Instead of worrying, pray. Let petitions and praises shape your worries into prayers, letting God know your concerns. 7 Before you know it, a sense of God's wholeness, everything coming together for good, will come and settle you down. It's wonderful what happens when Christ displaces worry at the center of your life.

**PHILIPPIANS 4:6-7, THE MESSAGE**

I can't believe our time together is over. I'm so proud of you and the work you've done. I'm so proud of your courage and honesty. This is only the beginning. Keep sharing your honest songs and your Psalm 40 stories to bring praise and glory to our good Father in heaven.

I want to leave you with a few parting words.

## MY CHARGE TO YOU

My charge to you today, and for as long as you have breath in your lungs, is this:

Tell the truth.

Settle it in your heart that God is good.

Trust Him in the pain.

Remember His salvation and how He has rescued you.

Tell the stories that make God known and knowable—the good stories and the hard stories.

## A PSALM 40 BENEDICTION

May you be weak and embrace your neediness.

May you be humble and embrace your poverty.

May you be patient and embrace wide-eyed wonder at what your God will do.

May you cry for help and embrace trust.

May you cry in lament and embrace the truth that what is wrong will one day be made right.

May you thank God in the pit and embrace the truth that God is with you and will deliver you.

May you accept God's offer of healing and embrace the difficult path it takes.

May you find strength in and on the Rock on which you stand and embrace your soul security.

May you be a singer of praise and embrace honest songs.

May you be a truth teller and embrace the story God has written for you.

May your life tell of what God has done and may you embrace the call to tell the generations.

Amen.

SESSION EIGHT:

# WRAP-UP

As for you, O LORD, you will not restrain
your mercy from me;
your steadfast love and your faithfulness will
ever preserve me!

**PSALM 40:11**

# GROUP GUIDE

## WARM THINGS UP

Here are a few questions to begin your time.

> When you think of the fear of the Lord, what comes to mind? Did our study of the topic this past week change your perspective at all? Discuss.

> What do you hope people see and hear when they look at and listen to you life?

> What does it mean to you that Jesus is your High Priest, making intercession for you before God the Father?

> If you feel comfortable, share the step of obedience (we discussed last session) that you feel God is calling you to take.

## WATCH

To view Session Eight's teaching from Sarah Mae, download the optional video bundle at LifeWay.com/Psalm40.

## CREATE CONVERSATION

> Discuss the Psalm 40 Charge and Benediction. Which pieces of it were encouraging to you? Which were challenging to you? Explain.

> What's one takeaway that you'll continue to use from our study of Psalm 40?

> Take a moment to celebrate! It might be fun to go around and honor the other women in the group, encouraging them with the ways you've seen God work in them. Feel free to write these encouragements down anonymously if you'd like. People can be bashful sometimes in situations like these.

Close your meeting by taking about ten minutes to pray, allowing anyone in the group to offer a prayer of praise. It can be like popcorn prayer! Praise God for your time together as a group. Pray for those who shared a step of obedience that they feel God is asking them to take.

*#PSALM40STUDY*

# APPENDIX

But may all who seek you
rejoice and be glad in you;
may those who love your salvation
say continually, "Great is the Lord!"

**PSALM 40:16**

# 6 WAYS TO FORGIVE

## (When You Don't Know What to Do with the Unfairness of It All)

1. **PRAY.** Say to God, "Lord, I feel like this situation is so unfair and I feel so wronged and I don't know what to do with it, but I trust that you do know what to do with it. You know me, you know them, and you see all the things I don't. Plus, I know you love me and have my back (as well as theirs), so here you go God, it's all yours." In other words, trust God with the person and the situation.

2. **REMEMBER.** Would you agree that life is hard? It is, and the fact is, nobody gets a free pass to skip the battle, not even the person who wronged you. When I remember that truth, that everyone is facing a hard battle, I can have compassion on the person who wronged me. Think also about all the times you have wronged someone. These considerations will help us to be more compassionate as well.

3. **ASK.** Is there something I have done that I should ask forgiveness for with the person who wronged me? Ask it. And ask without expectation that you will be asked for forgiveness in return. Free and clear, ask genuinely. Ask God to show you where you may have gone wrong or offended the other person.

4. **CHOOSE.** Choose to be a person of the light. I love this quote from Martin Luther King Jr. "Darkness cannot drive out darkness; only light can do that."[1] Lewis B. Smedes said, "To forgive is to set a prisoner free and discover that the prisoner was you."[2] The enemy wants nothing more than to keep you in the dark—seething, feeling vengeful, worked up, without peace—he wants you far away from forgiveness, because forgiveness shines blindingly, beautifully bright bringing glory to God. Set yourself free by forgiving

5. **SEEK.** Seek outside help from wise and kind mentors and/or counselors. God in His kind provision gives people gifts of counseling, and we can reap such healthy rewards through the help of others. I would not be where I am today if it weren't through the gentle help of so many others. Don't try to heal on your own.

**6. EVALUATE.** Evaluate the relationship you're in. Is it twisty and consuming, manipulative, unhealthy, and messed up? Take some time to honestly assess the situation and the relationship. You can forgive someone and still set boundaries or make a clean break if necessary. Pulling away for a time may be especially helpful and wise. It sometimes allows us to gets ourselves in a healthy place, so we can forgive and love well, whether that is up-close or from a distance.

$^{31}$ Let all bitterness and wrath and anger and clamor and slander be put away from you, along with all malice. $^{32}$ Be kind to one another, tenderhearted, forgiving one another, as God in Christ forgave you.

**EPHESIANS 4:31-32**

# BECOMING A CHRISTIAN

Romans 10:17 says, "So faith comes from hearing, and hearing through the word of Christ." Maybe you've stumbled across new information in this study. Or maybe you've attended church all your life, but something you read struck you differently than ever before. If you have never accepted Christ but would like to, read on to discover how you can become a Christian.

Your heart tends to run from God and rebel against Him. The Bible calls this *sin*. Romans 3:23 says, "for all have sinned and fall short of the glory of God."

Yet God loves you and wants to save you from sin, to offer you a new life of hope. John 10:10b says, "I came that they may have life and have it abundantly."

To give you this gift of salvation, God made a way through His Son, Jesus Christ. Romans 5:8 says, "but God shows his love for us in that while we were still sinners, Christ died for us."

You receive this gift by faith alone. Ephesians 2:8-9 says, "For by grace you have been saved through faith. And this is not your own doing; it is the gift of God, not a result of works, so that no one may boast."

Faith is a decision of your heart demonstrated by the actions of your life. Romans 10:9 says, "if you confess with your mouth that Jesus is Lord and believe in your heart that God raised him from the dead, you will be saved."

If you trust that Jesus died for your sins and want to receive new life through Him, pray a prayer similar to this to express your repentance and faith in Him:

> "Dear God, I know I am a sinner. I believe Jesus died to forgive me of my sins. I accept Your offer of eternal life. Thank You for forgiving me of all my sin. Thank You for my new life. From this day forward, I will choose to follow You."

If you have trusted Jesus for salvation, please share your decision with your group leader or another Christian friend. If you are not already attending church, find one that faithfully teaches God's Word, in which you can worship and grow in your faith. Following Christ's example, ask to be baptized as a public expression of your faith.

# RECOMMENDED RESOURCES

*Addictions: A Banquet in the Grave* by Edward T. Welch

*Afraid of All the Things* by Scarlet Hiltibidal

*Boundaries* by Henry Cloud and John Townsend

*Depression: Looking Up from the Stubborn Darkness* by Edward T. Welch

*Get Out of That Pit* by Beth Moore

*Kiss the Wave* by Dave Furman

*Recovering Redemption* Bible study by Matt Chandler

*Suffering and the Heart of God: How Trauma Destroys and Christ Restores* by Diane Langberg

*Suffering Is Never for Nothing* by Elisabeth Elliot

*Surrendering the Secret* by Pat Layton

*The Path of Loneliness* by Elisabeth Elliot

*The Question that Never Goes Away: Why?* by Philip Yancey

*Trusting God* by Jerry Bridges

# ENDNOTES

## Introduction

1. Eugene H. Peterson, *Answering God: The Psalms as Tools for Prayer* (New York: Harper Collins, 1991), 11.

## Session 1

1. "*Kardia*," Strong's 2588, HELPS Word-Studies, Bible Hub. Available at https://biblehub.com.
2. Howard Hendricks and William Hendricks, *Living by the Book* (Chicago, IL: Moody Publishers, 2007), 194.

## Session 2

1. "*Shavah*," Strong's 5594, *NAS Exhaustive Concordance*, Bible Hub. Available at https://biblehub.com.
2. Fuller Studio, "Bono & Eugene Peterson on THE PSALMS," (video), Available at https://fullerstudio.fuller.edu/bono-eugene-peterson-psalms/
3. William Paul Young, as quoted in Efrem Graham, "The Heart of Man: Heading to theaters again Oct. 17," Sept. 14, 2017, CBN News. Available at www1.cbn.com.
4. "*Homologeo*,"Strong's G3670, Blue Letter Bible. Available at www.blueletterbible.org.
5. Ralph P. Martin, *James, Word Biblical Commentary* 48 (Dallas: Word, 1990), 211.
6. W. N., "Coal," *The Jewish Encyclopedia, Volume IV* (New York: Funk and Wagnalls Co., 1903), 124.
7. Dr. Henry Cloud and Dr. John Townsend, *Boundaries: When to Say Yes, When to Say No to Take Control of Your Life* (Grand Rapids, MI: Zondervan, 1992), 269.
8. Jason Gray, "Is The Name Of God The Sound Of Our Breathing?" The Rabbit Room, August 19, 2011. Available at https://rabbitroom.com.
9. James David Audlin, *Breathing the Name of God: "YHWH" and "Elohim" in the Gospel of John, Volume II*, as published by Editores Volcan Baru, 2013. Available at www.academia.edu.
10. "Matthew 5:3" note, *ESV Study Bible* (Wheaton, IL: Crossway, 2008), 1827.
11. "*Ebyon*," Strong's H34, *Strong's Exhaustive Concordance*, Bible Hub. Available at https://biblehub.com.

## Session 3

1. "*Qavah*," Strong's H6960, Blue Letter Bible. Available at www.blueletterbible.org.
2. You can read the story of the relationship between my mom and me in my book, *The Complicated Heart* (B&H 2019).
3. "*Rahab*," *Holman Illustrated Bible Dictionary*, eds. Charles W. Draper, Chad Brand, and Archie England (Nashville, TN: Holman Reference 2003).
4. George Adam Smith, D. D., *The Expositor's Bible: The Book of Isaiah, Vol. 1, Isaiah I. I-XXXIX*, edited by Sir William Robertson Nicoll (New York: A. C. Armstrong and Son, 1908), 223–224.
5. "*Prasso*," Strong's G4238, Blue Letter Bible. Available at www.blueletterbible.org.

6. "*Saphad,*" Strong's 5594, *Strong's Exhaustive Concordance,* Bible Hub. Available at https://biblehub.com.

7. "*Alah,*" Strong's H5927, Blue Letter Bible. Available at www.blueletter-bible.org.

8. J. A. Thompson, "Sackcloth," *New Bible Dictionary,* 3rd edition, eds. D. R. W. Wood, I. H. Marshall, A. R. Millard, J. I. Packer, and D. J. Wiseman (Leicester, England; Downers Grove, IL: InterVarsity Press. 1996), 1032.

9. "What is the meaning of sack-cloth and ashes?" Got Questions Ministries. Accessed March 14, 2019. Available at www.gotquestions.org.

## Session 4

1. "*Abba,*" HELPS Word-Studies, Bible Hub. Available at https://biblehub.com.

2. "*Malak,*" Strong's 4397, *Strong's Concordance*, Bible Hub. Available at https://biblehub.com.

3. "Psalm 23," *Feasting on the Word,* Volume 6, eds. David Lyon Bartlett and Barbara Brown (Louisville, KY: Westminster John Knox Press, 2009), 432.

4. The Bible Project, "YHWH/LORD" (video). Available at https://thebibleproject.com/videos/yhwh-lord/

5. "Word Study: YHWH (God)," Chaim Bentorah Biblical Hebrew Studies, Sept. 2012. Available at www.chaimbentorah.com.

6. "Psalm 40:1," Gerald H. Wilson, *The NIV Application Commentary, Psalms, Vol. 1* (Grand Rapids, MI: Zondervan, 2002), 640.

7. "40:6-8" note, *HCSB Study Bible* (Nashville, TN: Holman Bible Publishers, 2010), 921.

8. David L. Allen, *The New American Commentary, Hebrews,* (Nashville, TN: B&H Publishing Group, 2010).

9. Ibid., 115.

10. William L. Lane, *Word Biblical Commentary, Vol. 47b, Hebrews 9-13* (Columbia: Word, Inc., 1991), 263.

11. Ibid., *The New American Commentary, Hebrews,* 498.

12. F.F. Bruce, *The Epistle to the Hebrews: New International Commentary on the New Testament,* Revised (Wm. B. Eerdmans Publishing, 1990).

13. Peter Craigie, *Word Biblical Commentary: Psalms 1–50* (Word, Inc., 1983).

14. Ibid., *HCSB Study Bible,* 921.

15. Ibid., *The NIV Application Commentary,* 640.

16. Yona Sabar, "Hebrew Word of the Week: hinneh," Jewish Journal, Nov. 10, 2016. Available at http://jewishjournal.com.

## Session 5

1. Fun Joel, "What Is … A Cistern?" Fun Joel's Israel Tours, Sept. 2, 2010. Available at http://funjoelsisrael.com.

2. "Cistern," *Holman Illustrated Bible Dictionary* (Nashville, TN: Broadman and Holman, 2010).

3. Amazing info and pictures of cisterns in Israel are available at https://biblewalks.com/Sites/Arumah.html.

4. "*Sha'own*," Strong's H7588, Blue Letter Bible. Available at www.blueletterbible.org.

5. "*Pronoia*," Strong's G4307, *Thayer's Greek Lexicon*, Bible Hub. Available at https://biblehub.com.

6. J. Andrew Dearman, "Chapter 38," *The NIV Application Commentary, Jeremiah and Lamentations* (Grand Rapids, MI: Zondervan, 2002), 324.

7. Jeremiah 38:6," F. B. Huey Jr., *The New American Commentary: Jeremiah, Lamentations* (Broadman Press, 1993), 334.

8. Phil Logan, "Cornerstone," *Holman Illustrated Bible Dictionary*, eds. Charles W. Draper, Chad Brand, and Archie England (Nashville, TN: Holman Reference 2003).

9. "Isaiah 28:16," *Ellicott's Commentary for English Readers*, Bible Hub. Available at https://biblehub.com.

10. John MacArthur, *The MacArthur Bible Commentary* (Nashville, TN: Thomas Nelson, 2005), 791.

11. "Isaiah 42:18," John N. Oswalt, *The NIV Application Commentary, Isaiah* (Grand Rapids, MI: Zondervan, 2003), 466.

12. Ibid.

### Session 6

1. Paige Patterson, *The New American Commentary, Revelation* (Nashville, TN: B&H Publishing Group, 2010).

2. Learn more about these major festive occasions from Cantor Lawrence, "Singing Hallel During Pesach," Congregation Beth Israel, April 3, 2014. Available online at www.youtube.com.

3. Steven J. Lawson, *Holman Old Testament Commentary, Psalms 76–150*, ed. Max Anders (Nashville, TN: Holman, 2006).

4. "*Hallel*," *Easton's Bible Dictionary*, Bible Hub. Available at https://biblehub.com.

5. Rabbi Baruch S. Davidson, "Why do we divide the Hallel into two at the Passover Seder?" Available at www.chabad.org.

6. Craig L. Blomberg, "26:26–30," *The New American Commentary: Matthew* (Nashville, TN: B&H Publishing Group, 2011). Retrieved from https://app.wordsearchbible.com.

7. Ibid.

8. Paraphrased from The 2000 Baptist Faith and Message. Available at www.sbc.net/bfm2000/bfm2000.asp.

9. *The NIV Application Commentary, Psalms, Vol. 1*, 278.

10. Nicholas Wolterstorff, *Lament for a Son* (Grand Rapids, MI: Wm. B. Eerdmans Publishing Co., 1987), 6.

11. Dana Gould, *Shepherd's Notes, Psalms 1-50* (Nashville, TN: Holman Reference, 1999).

12. Ibid., 137.

13. Ibid., 139.

14. "Psalm 27:7-12," Gerald H. Wilson, *The NIV Application Commentary, Psalms, Vol. 1.*

15. "Psalm 27:7-9" note, *CSB Study Bible* (Nashville, TN: Holman Bible Publishers, 2017), 840.

16. "Psalm 27:4," *Tyndale Old Testament Commentaries: Psalms* (2013), 151. Retrieved from https://app.wordsearchbible.com.

17. David W. Music, "Praise," *Holman Bible Dictionary*, gen. ed. Trent C. Butler (Nashville, TN: Holman Bible Publishers, 1991), 1130.

18. "*Tehillah*," Strong's 8416, *Strong's Exhaustive Concordance*, Bible Hub. Available at https://biblehub.com.

19. Joseph Hart, "Come, Ye Sinners, Poor and Needy," *Baptist Hymnal* (Nashville, TN: LifeWay Worship, 2008), 420.

## Session 7

1. *Holman Illustrated Bible Dictionary*, Chad Brand and Eric Mitchell, eds (Nashville, TN: B&H Publishing Group, 2015), 563.

2. Ibid.

3. "*Batach*," Strong's H982, Blue Letter Bible. Available at www.blueletter-bible.org.

4. "*Yare*," Strong's H3372, Blue Letter Bible. Available at www.blueletter-bible.org.

5. Rodney Combs, *Shepherd's Notes: 1, 2, 3 John* (Nashville, TN: Holman Reference, 2018), 66.

6. Ibid., "1 John 4:16" note, *ESV Study Bible*.

7. Ibid., "Proverbs 1:7" note.

8. Ibid.

9. Ibid.

10. Dave Furman, "If God Loves You, He Will Prune You," The Gospel Coalition, Feb. 28, 2018. Available at www.thegospelcoalition.org.

11. "*Elegcho*," Strong's G1651, Blue Letter Bible. Available at www.blueletterbible.org.

12. Ibid., *The NIV Application Commentary: Psalms Vol. 1*, 543.

13. "*Kalos*," Strong's G2570, *Strong's Concordance*, Bible Hub. Available at https://biblehub.com.

14. Ibid.

15. "Exodus 28:2" note, John MacArthur, *John MacArthur Bible Commentary* (Nashville, TN: Thomas Nelson), 123.

16. Ibid., "Exodus 28:2" note, *ESV Study Bible*.

17. Douglas K. Stuart, *The New American Commentary: Exodus* (Nashville, TN: Holman Reference, 2006).

18. Ibid., *Tyndale Old Testament Commentaries: Psalms* (2013), 230.

19. "*Azar*," Strong's H5826, Blue Letter Bible. Available at www.blueletter-bible.org.

## Appendix

1. Martin Luther King Jr., *Strength to Love* (Minneapolis, MN: Fortress Press, 2010), 47.

2. Lewis B. Smedes, "Forgiveness—The Power to Change the Past," *Christianity Today*, Dec. 1, 2002. Available online at www.christianity-today.com.

# Additional Studies on the Psalms

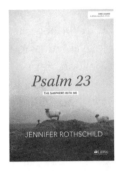

## PSALM 23
by Jennifer Rothschild
7 Sessions

Gain fresh insight and encouragement from one of the most familiar Psalms.

LifeWay.com/Psalm23

## STEADFAST LOVE
by Lauren Chandler
7 Sessions

Study Psalm 107 verse by verse to learn to face each season of life with courage and trust in Jesus.

LifeWay.com/SteadfastLove

## REDEEMED
by Angela Thomas-Pharr
7 Sessions

Pray through the Psalms to apply the concept of ongoing redemption in your life.

LifeWay.com/Redeemed

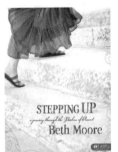

## STEPPING UP
by Beth Moore
7 Sessions

Journey through the Psalms of Ascent, Psalms 120–134, to experience a new level of intimacy with God.

LifeWay.com/SteppingUp